Simon & Schuster's

GUIDE TO

Horses & Ponies of the World

by
Maurizio Bongianni

Consultant Editor Jane Kidd

A FIRESIDE BOOK
PUBLISHED BY SIMON & SCHUSTER INC.
New York London Toronto Sydney Tokyo Singapore

Opposite title page: detail of an Assyrian relief from Nimrud, showing a Chaldean horseman in battle. British Museum, London.

Copyright © 1987 Arnoldo Mondadori Editore S.p.A., Milan
English translation copyright © 1988 Arnoldo Mondadori Editore S.p.A., Milan
Translated by Ardèle Dejey
Consultant editor Jane Kidd
Symbols by Grafica Service
Drawings by Piero Cozzaglio and Roberto Ricciotti

Simon and Schuster/Fireside Books,
Published by Simon & Schuster Inc.
Simon & Schuster Building
Rockefeller Center
1230 Avenue of the Americas
New York, New York 10020

SIMON AND SCHUSTER, FIRESIDE and colophons are registered trademarks of Simon & Schuster Inc.
Originally published in Italian under the title CAVALLI by Arnoldo Mondadori Editore S.p.A., Milan

Printed and bound in Spain by Artes Gráficas Toledo, S.A.
D.L.TO:1595–1993

10 9 8 7 6 5 4 3 2 1
10 9 8 7 6 5 4 Pbk.

Library of Congress Cataloging in Publication Data

Bongianni, Maurizio
  Simon & Schuster's guide to horses & ponies of the world.

  Translation of: Cavalli.
  Bibliography: p.
  Includes index.
  1. Horses. 2. Horse breeds. 3. Ponies.
  I. Title. II. Title: Guide to horses & ponies of the world. III. Title: Simon and Schuster's guide to horses and ponies of the world.
  SF285.B6713 1988 636.1 87-26434
  ISBN 0-671-66067-5
  ISBN 0-671-66068-3 (Fireside book: pbk.)

CONTENTS

PREFACE   page   7

INTRODUCTION   page 10

LIGHT DRAFT, PACK AND
SADDLE BREEDS   entries 1-85

HEAVY DRAFT BREEDS   entries 86-114

PONIES   entries 115-173

BREEDS NOT ILLUSTRATED   page 240

GREAT CHAMPIONS OF TODAY   page 242

BIBLIOGRAPHY   page 253

INDEX   page 254

PICTURE SOURCES   page 256

The Publisher wishes to thank the following individuals and associations, listed below, for their invaluable assistance and the photographic material they kindly supplied:

The American Albino Association, New York
Australian National University, Department of Prehistory and Anthropology, Faculty of Art, Canberra
Association Nationale du Poney Landais, Saubisse
Associazione Nazionale Allevatori Cavallo di Razza Maremmana, Grosseto
Associazione Nazionale Allevatori del Cavallo Agricolo Italiano da Tiro Pesante Rapido, Verona
Associazione Siciliana Allevatori di Equini (A.S.A.E.), Ragusa
Azienda Agricola di Nino Boscarelli, Cosenza
Bulgarian Embassy, Dr. Asen Marcevski, Rome
Mrs. Joanna Collard, Crows Nest (Australia)
Consejeria de Agricultura, Principado de Asturias, Spain
Department of Government Service, Nova Scotia
Direktorat Bina Produksi Peternakan, Jakarta
Don Antonio Ariza Cañadilla, Mexico
Dozsa S.K., Kiskunfelegyhaza
Edizioni Agricole Calderisi, Bologna
Mr. Kovacs, Hungarian Office of Commerce, Milan
Istituto Incremento Ippico della Sardegna, Ozieri
Dr. Jordan Ivanov, Milan
Mrs. Mary Johnson, Turin
Mrs Rosetta Lauria, Ragusa
Mr. Giovanni Lostia, Ozieri
Dr. Paolo Manili, Milan
Dr. J. Menegatos, Department of Animal Production, Agricultural College of Athens, Greece
Mini Ranch Iliade di Luigi Maraschi, San Giuliano Milanese
Ministério da Agricultura, Florestas e Alimentação, Lisbon
Dr. Giuseppe Pigozzi, Verona
Podere Torre Allevamento Quarter Horse di Adriano Simonazzi, Collecchio
Dr. Sabino Serra, Laboratoria Nacional de Investigaçao Veterinaria, Lisbon
Turkish Consulate, Milan

PREFACE

Throughout history much has been written on the subject of the horse, and I myself, through my books, have added modestly to the already vast literature on this wonderful animal. Many authors have sought to create a vivid image of the horse by classifying the different breeds in relation to their principal aptitudes, which generally reflect the morphological types to which they belong.

This book, too, is based on the same criterion and has a preliminary section dealing with matters of a general nature, followed by a larger section devoted to the description of the various breeds, with particular reference to the uses to which they can be put.

Breeds characterized by their functions as saddle, light draft, heavy draft, harness, coach or farm horses, while presenting a predominant aptitude for a certain type of work or sport, can, however, often be used to perform other rôles, though sometimes with less satisfactory results. The classification of breeds according to their morphology into dolichomorphic, mesomorphic and brachymorphic, and intermediate types, is, in my opinion, the most acceptable, and infinitely preferable to grouping them into warm- and cold-bloods, which distinction only indicates the degree of influence of the Arab. Dolichomorphic breeds are long-limbed and particularly suited to running and racing, mesomorphic breeds are more sturdy, with harmonious lines, and a powerful and rapid action making them good riding horses, suitable for light farm work, and brachymorphic breeds are more massive, compact, with predominantly short, strong lines, particularly suited to heavy draft and farm work. Besides grouping horses into the broad categories of saddle and light draft, heavy draft and ponies, I have therefore considered it useful to the reader to include an indication as to the morphological type of each individual breed.

In describing the conformation of each breed I have taken the liberty of including the shoulder with the parts of the body, rather than with the limbs.

This book, which is not intended as a learned treatise on the horse, but a general, and, as far as has been possible, exhaustive guide to the many different world breeds, aims to be of practical use to horselovers as well as to anyone who wishes to learn more about this beautiful and noble creature.

The Author

KEY TO SYMBOLS

flag of country of origin.

flat racing or
steeplechasing

harness racing (mounted)

show jumping, dressage,
eventing

high school

pony trekking

rodeo

polo

circus

herding

riding

harness racing
(trotting or pacing)

light draft or
medium-light draft

coach horse

historically used for drawing
stagecoaches or similar

heavy draft

farm work

pack horse

breed of international
importance

breed of national
importance

breed of regional or
local importance

breed in danger of
extinction

extinct breed

important in the development
of modern breeds

Abbreviations

b.	bay
bl.	black
br.	brown
c.	chestnut
d.b.	dark bay
gr.	gray
m.	male
f.	female

ORIGINS OF THE SPECIES

The horse is an ungulate mammal of the order *Perissodactyla*, family *Equidae*, genus *Equus* and species *caballus*. The *Perissodactyla* are four-legged animals characterized by their feet, which rest on an odd number of toes, either three or a single one (the middle toe) protected by a covering of horn, called a hoof.

The horse, *Equus caballus*, has evolved over a period of about sixty million years, starting in the early Tertiary era with *Eohippus*. From *Eohippus* in the Paleocene it developed via *Orohippus* and *Epihippus* of the Eocene and *Mesohippus* and *Miohippus* of the Oligocene into *Merychippus* during the Miocene, which stage in its evolution it reached either directly or via *Parahippus*. From *Merychippus* it further evolved during the Pliocene to become *Pliohippus* and eventually about one million years ago became recognizable as the genus *Equus*, the direct ancestor of *Equus caballus*, which first appeared during the Neolithic.

During this evolutionary process, over millions of years, many branches became extinct, as was the case with *Anchitherium* and *Hypohippus*, both of which descended from *Miohippus*, and *Hipparion* and *Hippidion*, which stemmed from *Merychippus*. The greater part of the evolution of the horse occurred on the American continent, from where *Equus* migrated to Asia, Europe and South America. *Hyracotherium*, the European contemporary of *Eohippus*, became extinct

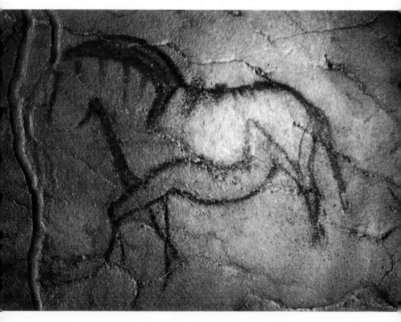

during the Eocene. In the late Pleistocene (about ten thousand years ago) the species living on the American continent disappeared, for reasons still unknown. The horse reappeared in America only after it was reintroduced to the continent by Christopher Columbus.

The evolution of the species has been accompanied by profound changes in stature, the shape of the molar teeth and the structure of the limbs. The height at the shoulder has gradually increased from about 9 in (24 cm) in Eohippus, to about 4 ft 4 in (1.3 m) in *Equus caballus*, which is similar in size to the present-day *Equus przewalskii poliakov*. As a result of changes in diet the molars slowly became more prismatic in shape and developed hard enamel ridges, suitable for grinding. The most important transformation occurred in the limbs and concerns the number of toes. *Eohippus* had four hoofed toes on each forefoot and three on each hind foot. In *Parahippus* this was reduced to three toes on all four feet, however, only one served to support the weight of the animal. In *Equus caballus* the number of toes was finally reduced to one only. The second and fourth digits still exist but only in vestigial form as thin, tapering splint bones (the secondary metacarpus and metatarsus, in the fore- and hind foot respectively, and the chestnut on all four legs.

All present-day horses can be traced back to three main progenitors, belonging to a single species. These are *Equus przewalskii gmelini*, otherwise known as the Tarpan, the now-extinct horse of the eastern European steppes, *Equus przewalskii poliakov* from Mongolia, also in danger of becoming extinct, and *Equus robustus* of Central Europe, the first of the three to die out. The lighter-built dolichomorphic and mesomorphic breeds descend from the first two while the brachymorphic type of central and southern Europe descends from the third.

THE FORMATION OF THE BREEDS

Any animal species may be subdivided into a number of natural or artificial breeds, that is groups of individuals sharing certain distinctive characteristics (breed standards), which are hereditarily transmissible. Natural breeds are formed by a process of natural selection, by which those individuals best adapted to a given environment succeed in surviving, passing on to their descendants their distinguishing characteristics. Most of today's breeds, however, are artificial, that is created by man in an attempt to perpetuate the most desirable characteristics of an individual. Artificial selection is therefore based on crossbreeding individuals belonging to different breeds, and hybridization, which is the coupling of crossbreds, that is those individuals obtained by crossbreeding. In artificial selection the choice of breeding stock is based either on morphological features (morphological selection) or functional characteristics (functional selection). In some cases, where functional selection prevails, the morphological

*A cave painting showing a horse, dating
from the mid Magdalenian period. Le Portel
cave (Ariège, France).*

characteristics become less well-defined and more variable, as in many racing breeds; in other cases, morphological selection is more important with the resultant enhancement of the distinctive physical characteristics of the breed.

REPRODUCTION AND REARING

Although the horse manifests the sexual instinct when it is nearly one year old, and reaches puberty at the age of two, it is inadvisable to mate either the male or the female before the age of three. The sexual life of horses is long, extending beyond the fifteenth year in stallions, and almost for life in the mare. The mare is able to reproduce throughout the year, but sexual activity is more pronounced in the period from February through August (northern hemisphere), with a high point during April, May and June. In this period, known as the breeding season, the sexual stimulus is more accentuated and the heat period in the female more evident. During this time the stallion may cover up to two mares a day. The mare's heat period lasts for three to eight days; in the event of no fertilization being achieved, it returns after three to four weeks, the oestrus cycle being of twenty-two days duration. In the female, the period of oestrum is accompanied by erection of the clitoris, reddening of the vaginal

mucus, and emission of a viscous fluid from the vulva; the mare frequently assumes the urinating position, lifts her tail, appears restless and shows a tendency to kick. The stallion reacts to a mare on heat by appearing agitated and excited, whinnying insistently and often presenting the sexual organ in erection.

The choice of breeding stock is based on artificial selection, which should take into account both the conformation and functional characteristics of the mare and the stallion. The selection of race horses for breeding takes place on the racecourse, through special competitions known as pattern races.

The first indications that a broodmare is in foal will become evident very soon after her final service: she will be noticeably quieter and show an increase in appetite, the udders will grow larger and after the fifth month the abdomen will begin to swell, assuming a more rounded appearance. The pregnancy has an average duration of eleven months and ten days; during this time the mare should not be subjected to rigorous work, however nor should she be left totally inactive and moderate exercise is advisable. During the last month of gestation this should be limited to a daily walk, or being let out in the field. At the approach of parturition the first warning signs appear: the mare is restless, her gaze becomes anxious and distressed, the udders become swollen and the animal alternately stands up and lies down at frequent intervals. At this point labor commences; the lips of the vulva open revealing the water bag, the breaking of which and the release of its viscous fluid assure the lubrication of the birth canal. From this moment the delivery period begins in which dilation of the neck of the uterus takes place and the contractions begin, becoming progressively stronger and more frequent. The phase is short and, in normal circumstances, the foal's two forelegs will appear soon after the water bag has made its appearance. After a short time and a few more contractions the foal's head appears. Once the shoulders are

The moment of capture for a horse on the Xilimhot plain in Mongolia.

through the foal slides out comparatively easily and the birth is completed.

One month after foaling the mare may resume normal activity. Heat recurs within a few days of foaling, during which period she is particularly fertile and may be covered again. The foal is suckled for about six to seven months after which it is weaned. In the wild this delicate transition takes place naturally under the mother's close supervision, however, foals born in captivity are generally completely separated from the mare as soon as they are considered old enough for training to begin.

BREAKING-IN AND WORK

Thoroughbreds destined for the racecourse are broken in at about eighteen months, however, with other breeds it is normal to wait until 2½ or 3½ years of age. Breaking a horse in is a very delicate operation and should be undertaken calmly and patiently, with no violence or maltreatment, seeking to persuade rather than to coerce. If these guidelines are not followed the animal may suffer mental trauma, which can have negative repercussions later. The human must seek to cultivate a feeling of trust and security in the animal to render it docile and calm. The young horse should be introduced to work very gradually and great care should be taken not to overexert it as this may make it unwilling to accept its new situation, or even reject it. A reasonable amount of work will help the physical development of the young animal while excessive fatigue will cause loss of appetite and consequent weakening that will impede its growth.

The horse should be put to the kind of work that best suits its build and aptitudes. Other factors that should also be taken into consideration are the sex and age of the animal, as well as climatic and seasonal conditions. Females tend to be more delicate than males and on hot days will become irritable; stallions are more attractive in appearance than geldings, but generally less even-tempered. Heat, especially if accompanied by a high level of humidity, makes work less acceptable, while wind irritates horses and makes them nervous. The seasons, too, can affect the animal's performance: in spring the horse is more lively and full of energy, while in summer, especially in hotter countries, its appetite diminishes and it endures its work with more effort, besides which, it is often bothered by insects. Fall is a transitional season during which the horse still feels the negative influences of summer; then in winter it regains it vitality, its appetite increases and the cold stimulates it to move more energetically.

SHOEING

A horse's hoof grows continually and will renew itself completely over a period of about nine months. In the wild, with soft pasture land and natural terrain under foot, there is a perfect balance between the rate at which the hoof wears down and the rate at which it regrows. Domestic animals, however, are often forced to walk long distances over very hard surfaces, such as roads and rough dirt tracks, frequently carrying or pulling heavy loads, and this subjects the hoof to an excessive rate of wear that is not naturally compensated for. If the horse is to be prevented from going lame as a consequence, steps have to be taken, the most efficient of which is shoeing, whereby a protective iron is applied to the underside of the hoof.

The practise of shoeing was probably originated by the ancient Germanic Cimbrian tribe as long ago as 1600 B.C., although some Oriental peoples may have used a form of horseshoe in even earlier times. The Romans shod their horses with a type of nailless horseshoe, or *solea*, which consisted of an iron plate attached to the underside of the hoof by means of clamps and leather straps. The modern horseshoe, which is fixed to the hoof with nails, dates back to the Middle Ages. Most horseshoes, even today, are still made of iron, although other materials such as aluminum and plastic are occasionally used, being lighter though less hardwearing.

As a shod hoof is protected and will not therefore wear down, the farrier or blacksmith must make sure that the hoof, which is growing constantly, is trimmed down to its original size every time the shoes are replaced (on average every thirty to forty days). The first shoeing is generally carried out soon after breaking-in, however care should be taken not to shoe a horse too early since this risks damaging the feet of a young animal.

Occasionally the horn of the front hooves will grow more quickly than that of the hind hooves, in which case only the forelegs should be reshod, and the hind legs left until the next shoeing.

The hoof is composed of a sloping outer wall of horn and on the underside the sole and frog. The wall can be subdivided into a forward area (the toe), symmetrical lateral sections the parts of which, from front to back, are known as the toe quarter and the heel quarter, and the heel at the rear. The height of the wall decreases from the toe

Shoeing horses in a blacksmith's forge, depicted in an English lithograph from the late nineteenth century.

to the heel, as does its outward slope; at the extremities of the heel the wall turns sharply inwards to form the two bars between which is the frog.

The sole of the hoof is composed of a thin layer of horny substance; its external surface is concave, and into this the wedge-shaped frog is inserted. The frog is composed entirely of horn, less compact than in the other parts of the hoof and with some elasticity that acts as a sort of shock absorber to the considerable pressures that are exerted on the foot as a whole. The frog is made up of an anterior section known as the apex, from which two branches run toward the rear divided by the central groove of the frog and terminating in the bulb of the heel.

The horny substance of which the hoof is formed is keratin, which, in the digital pad of the sole, forms an elastic structure that reduces the pressures exerted by the body weight. The bones that go to make up the foot of the horse are the lower half of the second phalanx (short pastern bone), the third phalanx (pedal bone), and the navicular bone.

The shoe is the same shape as the ground border of the hoof wall to which it is attached, and the different parts take the same names as the corresponding parts of the hoof, i.e. the toe, the toe quarters, the heel quarters and the heels. The shoe may also have projecting elements at the heels, bent downward and slightly forward, called calkins, the purpose of which is to provide a better grip on the ground, or extensions on the upper edge, turned upward, called clips, which ensure a more secure fit to the hoof wall. There may be either one single clip situated at the toe, or two clips, one at each toe quarter, and these may take different forms: triangular (Latin type) or semicircular (German type). In certain circumstances the clips may occasionally be used in place of nails. The shoes will differ in shape from the front hoof, which is more rounded, to the back, which is more oval with a more concave sole. Around the lower surface of the shoe runs a groove (the fullering) with rectangular holes through which the nails fixing the shoe to the hoof are driven. Generally there are eight nail holes, but some shoes have only five; according to whether they are set close to the outside edge or away from it they are said to be fine or coarse. In most European countries it is often the practise to leave the shoe somewhat proud of the edge of the hoof wall, but in Great Britain the shoe is usually filed back to the contours of the hoof. The upper surface of the shoe is also "seated out" to prevent the sole coming into contact with the shoe when the foot expands under the pressure placed on it.

Shoeing is an extremely skilled operation since, if badly done, it may affect the natural stance of the horse, adversely affecting its action. A good shoe should fit the hoof perfectly so that it is comfortable for the horse, and not too heavy. Shoeing may also have corrective or therapeutic uses, if, for example, a horse's natural stance is defective, or if there is pressure on the foot, or damage to the tendons. Obviously the fitting of special shoes will follow consultation with and approval by a veterinary surgeon.

PSYCHOLOGY

The horse, popularly depicted in literature and films as brave, courageous and hardworking, is in reality a nervous, apprehensive and lazy animal; it loves a quiet life and even years of domestication and training will fail to alter its true nature and sense of independence. Its submission to man is in fact no more than a compromise with itself that enables it to overcome its innate feelings of apprehension and insecurity. When frightened, a horse will often kick or bite, but in the face of real danger its most likely reaction will be to bolt. This flight mechanism is most evident in the seemingly heroic cavalry charge, in which horses are often credited with great bravery as they fling themselves headlong into the enemy lines. In fact, the horses are terrified by the shouts and bugle calls and, imagining the danger to be coming from behind, flee to what seems, in their panic, to be safety.

In spite of its timid and fearful nature, the horse shows an uncommon intelligence and sensitivity; fundamentally good-natured, it does not, however, easily forget cruelty, and even years later will remember everything that it associates with pain or suffering. Its relationship with man must be based on trust, and it is therefore important for the owner or trainer to be consistently firm and decisive, yet attentive and considerate, since the horse looks to him for protection. Horses, like humans, each present different subjective character traits that together form the personality. Thus a horse may be lazy, apathetic, generous, aggressive, nervous, curious, indifferent, obedient or obstinate. Horses are also capable of expressing a wide range of feelings such as love, hatred, jealousy, gratitude, like, dislike, and ill-will. It interprets man's wishes from the tone and inflection of his voice.

A horse's feelings toward fellow breeds are particularly evident in the wild state, where the animal is in a position to select for itself a group of individuals with which it can establish bonds of real friendship. The character of a race horse can generally be determined from its behavior on the track: there are competitive types that will fight to the last in order not to allow themselves to be beaten by an adversary. Others show themselves to be lazy and need constant encouragement, and then there are those that lose heart as soon as a competing horse overtakes them. Finally some horses always love to gallop or trot ahead of all the others and it will be a difficult task for the rider or driver to dampen their enthusiasm.

Horses express themselves and communicate with each other by making sounds: the whinny and the neigh. The whinny is a short, plaintive sound, low in tone, and always used to express distress; the neigh, however, presents itself in various forms denoting different situations and feelings. When long, high-pitched and repeated at regular intervals, the neigh conveys a sense of well-being and contentment; if the sounds are short and high-pitched they demonstrate anger; when the sound is drawn-out, ending with low repeated notes it expresses desire; if low-pitched, short and almost forced it denotes fear.

The horse's state of mind is also reflected by the position of the ears. When both ears are laid back flat, the animal can be expected to rebel, attack, or even bite. When the ears twitch backward and forward, independently of each other, they signal anger; when the horse is in movement, with one ear laid back and the other forward, but immobile, this indicates tension and may precede a show of obstinacy toward the rider or driver. Immobile ears that only move occasionally, with an accompanying movement of the head, convey insecurity and fear in the animal. Conversely, if they droop passively it shows that the horse is taking no interest in its surroundings, hearing sounds, but with indifference. Finally, when the horse is in movement, with its ears inclined slightly forward, in a proud and confident position, it denotes a sense of security and well-being.

Most horses are sociable toward other animals and will frequently have a kid goat, a dog or a cat as a constant stable companion. One famous example is the race horse, Diamond Jubilee, whose cat would even accompany it to the races, in the days before quarantine laws came into force. Some horses, however, display character defects that reduce their commercial value. Even after having been broken in, a horse may continue to defend itself by biting, kicking, stamping its feet, trying to scrape the rider's leg against a wall, or bolting. A bolting horse is trying to escape from the action of the reins on the bit, and will run away at full gallop to the extent of losing its own sense of self-preservation. This type of defect is generally found in anxious, nervous animals, with hard mouths, but may also be the result of back pain, or of a visual disturbance, such as a piece of white paper caught in a hedge.

Some vices consist of abnormal or unnatural means of defense

The horse is generally sociable with other animals, as is shown by this photograph taken on a golf course in Jamaica.

such as rushing a man, shying, rearing, not answering to the reins, making sudden sideways swerves in an attempt to unseat the rider, not allowing the rider to mount, or displaying awkward behavior once mounted. This category also includes touchy, restless or obstinate horses, such as those that back up, and those that try to crush the rider against a wall.

Other vices, all of which make the animal difficult to control, may be the consequence of bad habits such as constantly shaking the head; arching the neck and bowing the head down so the muzzle almost touches the chest; or holding the head too high to escape the action of the reins.

Finally there are some vices that are categorized as abnormal, as they denote either cunning or particular needs. Such vices include breathing in while being saddled in order to expand the girth, pawing at the ground, breaking loose from the halter, rubbing the tail, blowing the lips, lying down suddenly like a cow, lying down in water, lying down as soon as the harness is on, throwing fodder to the ground, eating excessive amounts of straw, putting the bit between the teeth, gnawing the blanket, kicking off the shoes, resting one foot on the other, and twitching. The last is always a sign of nervous tension, due sometimes to prolonged idleness, as is "weaving," when the head, neck and anterior parts of the body constantly swing from side to side, so that the weight rests alternately upon each forelimb. In bad cases the foot is raised as the weight passes over on to the other. This state can eventually deteriorate into a nervous disease and make the horse unsafe to ride. Another bad habit is "crib-biting" or "wind-sucking" in which the horse takes the edge of its manger or of

For horses, rubbing noses is a sign of friendship.

the door to its box between the teeth, emitting a characteristic sound caused by swallowing air.

GAITS

The natural gaits of the horse are the walk, the trot, the pace, the canter, and the gallop. In each of these gaits there are two distinct phases for each leg, the raising and putting down of the foot. The raising motion comprises the lifting of the foot from the ground, propulsion, and suspension, while the landing motion is accomplished in two stages, first the toe, followed fractionally by the heel.

In the walk, which is a regular gait of four separate beats, the horse moves its legs one at a time in the following order: right hind leg, left foreleg, left hind leg, right foreleg. This gait has the advantage of being very stable and comfortable for the rider as well as the horse, which can keep going steadily over long distances.

In the trot, which is a springing gait of two beats, the horse moves in a synchronized fashion. The legs move in diagonal pairs, first the right foreleg with the left hind leg, then the left foreleg with the right hind leg, or vice versa.

The canter is a fast gait of three beats, in which, the progression of movements is as follows: first one hind leg, then the other hind leg and the diagonally opposite foreleg together, and finally the remaining foreleg. At the canter, unlike the other gaits the back remains relatively rigid.

In the full gallop there are four beats because the movement of the one diagonal pair, which is synchronized in the canter, falls into two distinct beats.

The pace, like the trot, is a springing gait of two beats, but it is a lateral gait in which it is the two legs on the same side of the body that move together, first on one side, then the other.

WALK *A gait of four beats*

TROT *A springing gait of two beats*

PACE *The legs on the same side move simultaneously*

CANTER *A fast gait of three beats*

23

STANCES

A horse, besides having good conformation, should also have a correct "natural" stance. This means that when the animal is standing so the weight of the body is equally distributed over all four legs, there are no visible defects.

The stance is said to be correct when eight imaginary vertical lines leading respectively from the point of the shoulder (the scapulo-humeral joint), the mid point of the elbow, the point of the buttock, and the stifle (knee bone) on each side of the animal, present themselves in a precise relationship with the lines of the legs, showing that the horse's weight is being correctly carried. Verification of the correctness of the stance must be made by examination of the legs from the front (forelegs) and the back (hind legs) as well as from both sides of the animal.

Viewed from the side, the stance of the forelegs may be judged correct when the vertical line dropping from the point of the shoulder meets the ground about 4 in (10 cm) in front of the point of the toe, and the line from the elbow exactly bisects the knee, cannon and fetlock, meeting the ground just behind the heel. Viewed from the front the vertical from the point of the shoulder should exactly bisect the front of the elbow, knee, cannon, fetlock, pastern and foot. The stance of the hind legs is considered correct when, viewed from the side, the vertical from the point of the buttock just touches the point of the hock and continues down the back of the cannon, and the vertical line from the stifle meets the ground just in front of the point of the toe. Viewed from behind the vertical dropping from the point of the buttock should exactly bisect the hock, cannon, fetlock and foot.

Should the line of the legs in relation to the eight verticals deviate substantially from any of these guidelines, the stance must be considered incorrect; the horse may be thrust forward, under in front, forward at the knee, back at the knee, too narrow in front, too open at the front, pigeon-toed, splayed, with bow hocks, under at the back, straight-hocked, cow-hocked, sickle-hocked, narrow at the back, open at the back, short or long in the pastern.

Defects of stance will clearly have a negative effect on the performance of the animal at speed. A horse that is under in front will tend to stumble due to the legs knocking into each other (brushing); a horse that is thrust forward will have a restricted action and so will cover less ground; the hooves of a horse that is too close in front will tend to strike and damage the legs, especially whilst trotting; a splay-footed horse will tend to trip due to "dishing" where, during action the limbs are carried outward in a circular motion; a pigeon-toed horse will tend to brush itself especially at the trot and at the gallop; a horse that is too open at the front will generally develop a rolling gait and the soles of the feet will become bruised.

FORELIMBS
Front view

1 Correct natural stance
2 Too close or narrow in front
3 Too open in front
4 Pigeon-toed
5 Splayed or turned out

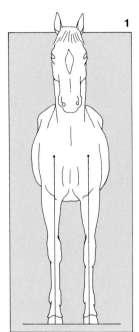

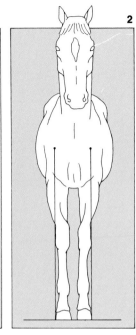

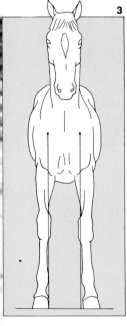

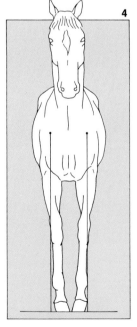

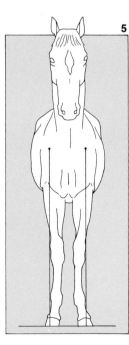

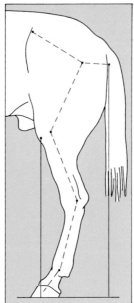
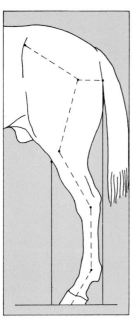

1 Correct natural stand
2 Under at the back
3 Straight hocks
4 Sickle hocks

HINDQUARTERS Side view

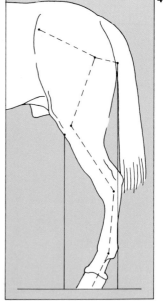
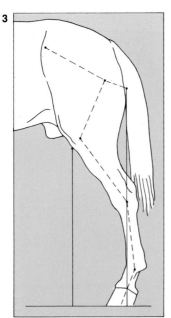

HINDQUARTERS
Rear view

1 Correct natural stance
2 Narrow at the back
3 Open at the back
4 Cow hocks
5 Bow hocks

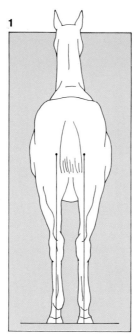

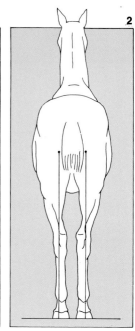

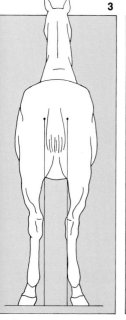

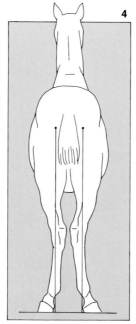

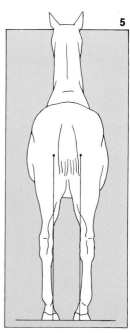

FORELIMBS Side view

1

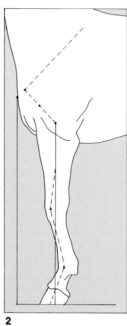

2

1 Correct natural stance
2 Over at the knee
3 Back at the knee
4 Thrust forward
5 Under in front

Opposite:

1 Front leg long and
  sloping
2 Hind leg long and
  sloping
3 Front leg short and
  upright
4 Hind leg short and
  upright

3

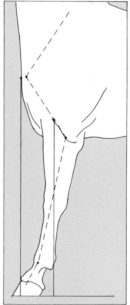

4

5

DEFECTS IN THE INCLINATION OF THE PASTERN IN THE FRONT AND HIND LEGS

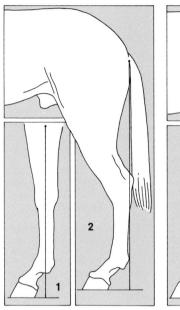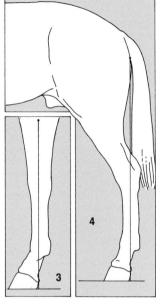

COATS

The hair covering the body of the horse is commonly known as the coat. Besides protecting the animal from adverse weather conditions, the coat provides an important means of identification, making it possible to distinguish between two horses of the same breed with almost total accuracy. The most obvious means of recognition is the color of the coat, however, when it is necessary to distinguish one horse from several similar colored horses of the same sex and breed, certain individual peculiarities and markings are taken into account. While the color of the coat may be subject to variations after a foal is born (in many cases the color of a foal's coat will differ from its adult coat, although it is usually possible to see what the adult coloring will eventually be from the color of the head) the markings on the coat are more permanent and less likely to alter. As well as modifications that come with age, the coat undergoes seasonal changes; in summer, when the animal molts, it is less thick and made up of shorter hairs, often causing it to vary slightly in color; in winter it is longer and thicker and where the climate is more rigorous takes on the look of fur. Different shades of the same color may occur in the same coat. When a coat is entirely composed of hairs of one color it is described as "whole colored" (cream, chestnut, or black). Other coats may be composed of hairs of two separate colors, such as bay, palomino, yellow dun, and blue dun; a mixture of hairs of two colors interspersed, as in red roan and gray; a mixture of three colors (roan);

it may have patches of hairs of a different color from the main body color (piebald and skewbald).

In a whole-colored coat there is no admixture of white hairs. When such an admixture occurs with bay, chestnut, black or palomino, the resultant color is called roan. A coat with circular markings of the same color as the body bolor, but differing in shade, is said to be "dappled."

White markings on the head take various names according to their shape and size. The *star* is a white, irregularly shaped mark, situated on the forehead, and varying considerably in size. When a star is prolonged downward along the nose it is said to be *extended*. The *stripe* is a narrow, white marking, regular or irregular, running down the length of the face as far as the nostrils. When there is a broader splash of white covering much of the forehead between the eyes and running down the nose toward the muzzle, the horse is said to have a *blaze*. In a *white face* the white covers the forehead and front of the face down to the muzzle; according to whether all or half of the face is covered the extension is said to be bilateral or unilateral. A *white muzzle* is where the white covers one or both lips and extends up to the nostrils.

A *snip* is a pink marking covered with soft down between the nostrils. *Fleshmarks* are areas of skin devoid of pigmentation and are found in places not covered by hair, such as the lips and the nostrils. An *eel stripe* or *list* is a black line running along the spine from the withers to the base of the tail.

A horse will frequently have white markings on the lower parts of the leg, known as socks or stockings, and these can vary considerably from a narrow band above the coronet to white socks reaching as high as the fetlock, the quarter cannon, the half cannon, the hock etc. Such markings may occur on one, two, three, or all four legs.

Other details of the coat are whorls, whirlpool-like formations of hair that prove very useful in identification, especially in the case of animals entirely devoid of other markings. A coat may also present the so-called zebra markings, horizontal black stripes found on the legs, especially of some of the more primitive breeds. For identification purposes, certain individual peculiarities play an important rôle; these are called "acquired" or "adventitious" markings, and occur as groups of white hairs resulting from wounds, bruises, grazing, or from pressure from the saddle or other parts of the harness; scars and brands also fall into this category. Other peculiarities, although unrelated to the coat, can also aid identification: the "Prophet's thumb mark," which is a muscular depression usually found at the base of the neck, sometimes in the shoulder and, more rarely, in the hindquarters, is one such peculiarity, more often found in Arabs and Thoroughbreds than in other breeds.

SIMPLE COATS (of one single color)

White: white hair on pink skin
- brilliant (*dazzling*)
- silver (*metallic tinge*)
- porcelain (*bluish tinge*)
- dirty (*yellowish tinge*)

Black: black hairs
- pure (*uniform*)
- dull (*slightly reddish*)
- raven (*dark and glossy*)

Chestnut: yellow to red hairs
- light (*red tending toward yellow*)
- golden (*gold-colored hair*)
- liver (*tending toward brown*)
- bloodstone (*tending toward maroon*)
- bronze (*bronze-colored hair*)
- mealy (*pale and washed out*)

COMPOSITE COATS
(two colors interspersed)

1 **Red roan:** white and red or yellow hairs
- light (*predominantly white*)
- dark (*predominantly red or yellow*)

2 **Gray:** white and black hairs, sometimes with an admixture of red
- light (*predominantly white hairs*)
- dark (*predominantly black hairs*)
- steel (*glossy with a predominance of black hairs*)
- silver (*glossy with a predominance of white hairs*)
- flecked (*predominantly black hairs with occasional clusters of white*)
- dappled (*with clearly defined patches of white hair*)
- flea-bitten (*small, scattered patches of black hairs*)

- pinkish (*admixture of red hairs*)
- white (*white hairs on black skin*)

COMPOSITE COATS
(with two separate colors)

3 **Yellow dun:** dark yellow hairs, black points
- mouse: (*dark yellowish color*)

4 **Dun:** yellow hairs down as far as the knees and hocks; black below the knees and hocks, tail and mane black)
- light (*tending toward white*)
- bright/cream (*tending toward yellow*)
- golden/palomino (*more glossy yellow*)

5 **Blue dun:** lead-colored hairs, black points; black mane and tail
- light
- dark

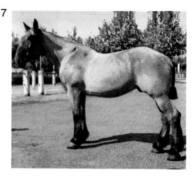

6 **Bay:** reddish hairs, black points; mane and tail black
- brown (*almost black*)
- dark (*brownish red*)
- chestnut (*brownish chestnut*)
- cherry (*color of a ripe cherry*)
- golden (*with golden highlights*)
- light (*faded color*)
- washed out (*muzzle, underbelly, flanks, and the inside of the thighs almost white*)

COMPOSITE COATS
(three colors)

7 **Roan:** white, red and black hairs
- light (*predominantly white*)
- dark (*predominantly black hairs*)
- chestnut (*predominantly red*)

**PIEBALD AND SKEWBALD
(irregular patches of hairs of two colors)**

Piebald: large, irregular patches of black and white
Skewbald: patches of white and any other color except black
Odd-colored: large patches of more than two colors

HEAD MARKINGS

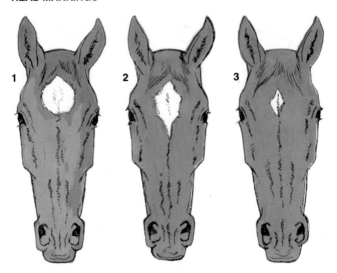

1 and 2 **Star** (can be any shape: round, oval, half-moon, crescent, pear, heart, irregular, triangular, polygonal, curved, oblique, linear)
3 **Small star** in middle of forehead
4 **Stripe** (can be irregular, asymmetric, curved, interrupted, inclined to left or right)
5 **Star and stripe conjoined**

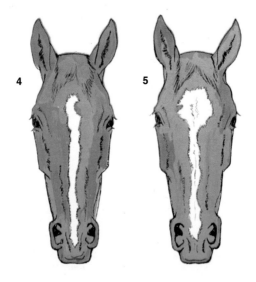

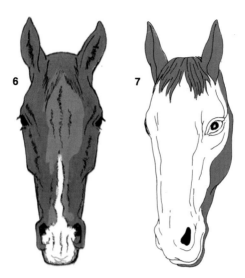

6 **White muzzle** (where white markings cover both lips and extend to nostrils. A "snip" is limited to the nostrils only).
7 **White face** (extension may be unilateral or bilateral).

WHITE LEG MARKINGS (socks or stockings)

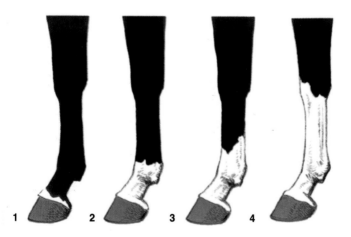

1 White band above coronet   3 White mark to half cannon
2 white mark to quarter cannon 4 White mark to hock

PECULIARITIES OF THE COAT

- **Whorl**

- **Herring-bone whorl**

DOMESTICATION AND EVOLUTION

All modern horses descend from the original breeds that first attracted the attention of primitive man, many thousands of years ago. It is not known exactly when the horse was first domesticated, nor by which ancient peoples, and a certain amount of controversy surrounds the issue. Some theorists believe that the Aryans or Scythians, ancient nomadic tribes, were the first to train horses and use them as mounts as early as the twentieth century B.C., whereas according to others the Chinese began domesticating horses very much earlier, in around 3500 B.C.

Whatever the exact date, however, there is no doubt that it marked the beginning of a relationship between horses and man that has lasted into the present day. To begin with horses would have been used for riding and as pack animals, but later, with the invention of the wheel, methods were devised of attaching the horse to carts by means of a primitive harness. Thus the strong and enduring draft breeds developed, capable of drawing coaches of people and wagons of goods over long distances that would have been impossible on foot. This facilitated trade and cultural exchanges between peoples from different geographical regions, and broadened man's horizons.

As the horse participated in the development and civilization of mankind, so man has contributed to the evolution of the horse, gradually modifying its morphological characteristics, by selective breeding, to suit his own requirements. Many breeds were formed, and although many others became extinct, they were able to pass on

some of their characteristics, directly or indirectly to newer breeds.

Machines have now taken over most of the jobs that horses traditionally carried out in agriculture, transport and in war, causing the disappearance of a number of purely functional breeds that were unable to adapt to the new mechanized society. Unfortunately, the survival of many other breeds has only been possible as a result of the dedication of a few breeders. Today the future of the horse lies in sports such as flat racing, trotting racing, polo, and eventing, as well as in leisure riding, which is steadily increasing in popularity.

Opposite: a carriage drawn by a team of four Lipizzaners. Below: for centuries horses have provided the main source of labor in a variety of different rôles, especially farm work.

FUNCTIONS

With the advent of motorization tasks that had for centuries been traditionally carried out by horses have gradually been undertaken by machines. This is particularly noticeable in the military, where the cavalry was very quickly substituted by battalions of tanks and armored vehicles. Similarly in transport and agriculture the change that occurred over little more than half a century was radical. Stagecoaches disappeared from the roads, and in the cities horse-drawn omnibuses became an increasingly rare sight, as these means of transport were rapidly replaced by faster, motorized vehicles.

Very soon the only area left solely to the horse was that of sport and leisure. Horse breeding thus became dedicated to the production of racing breeds (both trotting and flat racing), polo ponies, and competition horses. Many breeds that were used at one time in mountainous areas for agricultural work, are now used for riding holidays, where people can escape from the stresses of the city and rediscover a more humane way of life that brings them closer to nature. As a result, riding schools have sprung up everywhere to teach the increasing number of people who are becoming interested

in this new leisure activity, the rudimentary skills of horse riding.

Other breeds, once famous for drawing luxurious coaches and carriages, are gradually adapting to the changed environment and generally make good competition horses suited to a wide variety of equestrian events. Breeds that in the past were of the heavier, mesomorphic type have tended to become lighter, taller and more of the dolichomorphic type, acquiring different features, more in accordance with the demands of their new rôle. Some breeds disappeared altogether because they were unable to adapt to the new circumstances. Many breeds, although no longer used for the work for which they had been created continue to exist through the love of some inspired breeders. As in the past, all the breeds in existence today present particular morphological characteristics that relate to the functions they are requested to perform. However, it is not enough purely to belong to a specific breed, and in fact, only animals possessing the characteristics required for the fulfillment of the tasks they are called on to perform can be successfully employed. If a horse presents defects that restrict its performance of a given task, it will not prove practical to use it, even if it belongs to a suitable breed.

Use	Qualities	Temperament	Neck
Light draft	elegance, speed and endurance	calm but lively	in proportion and well-muscled
Slow heavy draft	endurance	willing	short and muscular
Fast heavy draft	speed and endurance	calm but energetic and lively	short and muscular
Farm work	endurance	willing	short and muscular
Polo	quick off the mark	well-balanced	in proportion and well-muscled
Hunting	agility, speed and stamina	energetic and lively	long and well-muscled
Classical horsemanship	elegance	calm	in proportion and well-muscled
Trotting racing	speed and stamina	well-balanced but highly strung	long and well-muscled
Steeplechasing	speed and stamina	well-balanced but highly strung	long and well-muscled
Flat racing	speed and stamina	well-balanced but highly strung	long and well-muscled
Show jumping	agility	well-balanced	long and well-muscled
Dressage	elegance	well-balanced	long and well-muscled
Eventing	agility and stamina	well-balanced	long and well-muscled
Long distance riding	stamina	calm and reliable	in proportion and well-muscled
Riding schools	endurance	calm and reliable	in proportion and well-muscled
Riding holidays	endurance	calm and reliable	in proportion and well-muscled

Shoulder	Limbs	Body	Defects
long and sloping	in proportion and well-muscled	broad chest; wide, deep girth; short, straight back; muscular croup	poor natural stance
straight and powerful	short and solid; short cannon and pastern; broad foot; well-developed quarters	broad, powerful chest; wide girth; short back; broad, muscular croup	small, fragile foot
long and powerful; sloping	short and well-muscled; short cannon and pastern; broad foot; well-developed quarters	broad, powerful chest; wide girth; short back; broad, muscular croup	small, fragile foot
straight and powerful	short and solid; short cannon and pastern; broad foot; well-developed quarters	broad, powerful chest; wide girth; short back; broad, muscular croup	small, fragile foot
long and sloping	in proportion and well-muscled	broad chest; short, straight back; muscular croup	defective natural stance
long and sloping	long and well-muscled	broad chest; wide, deep girth; long, straight back; muscular croup	defective natural stance
long and sloping	solid and well-muscled	broad chest; wide, deep girth; long, straight back; muscular croup	defective natural stance
long and sloping	long and well-muscled; long forearm; short cannon; nicely sloping pastern	broad chest; wide, deep girth; long, straight back, muscular croup	long cannon; short back
long and sloping	long and well-muscled; nicely sloping pastern	broad chest; wide, deep girth; short, straight back; muscular croup	long pasterns; weak tendons
long and sloping	long and well-muscled; nicely sloping pastern; small solid foot	broad chest; wide, deep girth; long, straight back; muscular croup	narrow chest and girth; long pasterns; weak tendons
long and sloping	long and well-muscled; nicely sloping pastern	broad chest; wide, deep girth; quite long, straight back; muscular croup	long pasterns; weak tendons
long and sloping	long and well-muscled	broad chest; wide, deep girth; long, straight back; muscular croup	poor conformation
long and sloping	long and well-muscled; nicely sloping pastern; strong tendons	broad chest; wide, deep girth; long, straight back; well-muscled croup	weak tendons
long and sloping	solid and well-muscled	broad chest; wide, deep girth; long, straight back; well-muscled croup	weak tendons; fragile limbs
long and sloping	solid	broad chest; wide, deep girth; long, straight back; well-muscled croup	fragile limbs; temperamental
long and sloping	solid and muscular	broad chest; wide, deep girth; long, straight back; well-muscled croup	fragile limbs; temperamental

LIGHT DRAFT, PACK AND SADDLE BREEDS

1 ARAB

Breed Arab or Arabian horse.
Place of origin Saudi Arabia.
Aptitudes Riding horse, light draft.
Qualities Speed and endurance, gentle and undemanding.
Temperament Highly strung.
Conformation An elegant horse of the mesomorphic type. The height at the withers varies from 14 to 15 hands (1·45–1·55m), although in some cases it may fall below the lower limit. The weight ranges from 840–990 lb (380–450 kg). Its coat may be gray, bay, chestnut, black or, more rarely, roan. It has a small head, with a straight or slightly dished profile, a broad forehead, small, alert ears, large expressive eyes, flared nostrils and fine lips. The neck is long and crested, broad at the base and well set-on to the body, with a thick mane; the withers are prominent and clearly defined, the back straight and short (the Arab has 17 thoracic vertebrae instead of the usual 18), the loins short (there are only 5 lumbar vertebrae instead of 6) and broad, the croup broad and flat, the tail full, set-on high, and carried with elegance, the chest well-muscled, broad and deep, the abdomen rather tucked up, and the shoulder long and sloping. The legs are well-muscled, with broad joints, the tendons clearly defined and prominent, and the foot small, with very tough horn. The conformation is perfect; the skin appears thin and elastic, and is covered with short silky hairs.
History The purebred Arab is one of the oldest breeds, and proof of its existence before the year 3000 B.C. is given by archeological finds that have come to light in the deserts of Saudi Arabia. A whole aura of mystery and mysticism surrounds this horse, about which a web of legends has been woven. According to one of these, the Arab is descended from seven original ancestors, selected by King Solomon from the forty thousand chariot horses and twelve thousand riding horses that he owned. From these seven steeds, so the legend goes, seven breeds were subsequently produced: Koheilan (with eyelids that look painted), Manaki (of the superb neck), Hedregi (energetic and tireless), Saklani (brave and intelligent), Gilfi (swift and powerful), Hedban (noble and valiant), and Trefi (proud). Popular tradition, however, claims that the Arab descends from the five mares of Muhammad that were the first to reach Mecca out of a total of eighty-five sent by the Prophet to bring news of the victory. According to the Raswaan, the foremost authority on the subject, there are three basic types of Arab: the Assil or Kocklani, the purebred Arab, and the Arab breed. The Assil, which also came to be described by different tribes as Kohuail, Koheil, Khamsa or Kamsat, is said to be the true Bedouin Arab. It can be classified into three sub breeds: the Kuhailan, symbol of endurance, the Siglavy, the image of beauty and elegance, and the Muniqi, the ultimate expression of speed. In comparison with the others, the Muniqi tends to be more elegant in appearance and has longer limbs, a longer neck and back, and a straight profile. It is said that the purebred Arab is the result of crossing the three main sub breeds, whereas the Arab breed includes animals whose precise origins are uncertain, or whose pedigrees reflect the influence of the Berber, the Persian, the Syrian, the Egyptian Arab, and other related breeds. The harmony and elegance of the lines make this breed indisputably the most beautiful in the world. It is for this reason that it has, in the past, been used internationally in the creation or improvement of many other breeds, in particular the English Thoroughbred.

2 BARB

Breed Barb.
Place of origin North Africa (Algeria and Morocco).
Aptitudes Riding horse.
Qualities Fast, resistant, frugal.
Temperament Docile, courageous.
Conformation An athletic horse of the mesomorphic type, whose height at the withers varies between 14 and 15 hands (1·45–1·55 m). The coat may be bay, brown, black chestnut or gray. The head is rather long, with pronounced jaws, a straight or convex profile, lively eyes, and flared nostrils. The neck is of medium length, well-muscled, and arched; the withers are prominent, the back short and straight, the quarters sloping, the tail low-set and flowing, the chest wide and deep, and the shoulder long and sloping. The legs are slender and solid, with broad joints, the cannons long, the tendons prominent and clearly defined, and the feet small, with tough horn.
History The history of the Barb runs parallel with that of the North African Berber people who have contributed greatly to its development. The breed was most probably introduced into Europe in the eighth century, at the time of the Moorish invasion of Spain, where it gave rise to the Andalusian. It has also been claimed, although wrongly, that the Godolphin Arabian (1724), which made a decisive contribution to the creation of the English Thoroughbred, was in fact a Barb and not an Arab as the name would suggest. In the seventeenth century the Barb was widely renowned throughout Europe, however, two centuries earlier in the streets of Rome it had taken part in the "corse dei Berberi," the famous Berber horse race of which Pope Paul II was the patron. Today it is reared as a purebred only among the nomadic populations of North Africa. Elsewhere the breed has been subjected to crosses with the English Thoroughbred, or the Arab as in the case of the Libyan Barb.

In the seventh century, when the Arabs invaded northern Africa, imposing their language, religion and culture on the local Berber peoples, the Barb was subjected to repeated crossings with Arab horses. The animals produced were of such high quality that they gradually substituted the original Barb, which consequently went into a decline. Toward the mid nineteenth century purebred Barbs had become so rare that they could only be found among remote tribes in the mountains and desert of Morocco. The true Barb therefore comes originally from Barbary, a geographical area, corresponding to present-day Algeria, Morocco, Tunisia, and Libya.

The Barb is the most hardy of all the Oriental breeds and proves particularly resistant to changes in climate, fatigue, and disease. It develops late and does not reach maturity until its sixth year. In the past this horse was highly prized as a war horse both by the Tuaregs in its native Africa, and in Europe.

The Tuaregs, a fearsome nomadic tribe, were the only Berbers successfully to defend their extensive territories from the Arab invasions, consequently the Barb horses they bred remained uncontaminated by the Arab. This proud people is renowned for the skill of its horsemen and the quality of the horses used in its warring forays.

3 PERSIAN ARAB

Breed Persian Arab.
Place of origin Iran.
Aptitudes Riding horse.
Qualities Fast with stamina.
Temperament Spirited, energetic.
Conformation A strong horse of athletic build; standing 14·1–15·1 hands (1·45–1·53 m) at the withers; the coat is usually bay, chestnut or gray, rarely black. Although considerably more robust in build, in the shape of the head and general lines the Persian Arab closely resembles the Arab, of which it can be considered a variety, presumably having common origins or being derived from it.
History The Persians (Iranians) have always imported Arab horses from the Negev to supplement and improve their breeding; according to their parentage the resulting progeny is called Hoor if both parents are Arab, Beradi if only the mother is Arab, and Hedijn if only the father is Arab. In Iran there are two breeds derived from the Persian and therefore also of Arab type: the Darashouri from the Fars region, and the Jaf from Kurdistan. Both have Arabian characteristics and stand about 15 hands (1·52 m) high. The coat varies from chestnut to bay or gray while black is rare. Both breeds are spirited horses, and have good stamina. Although the Jaf is more highly regarded, being used to harsh desert conditions, the Darashouri is more elegant. Another breed that should be mentioned is a halfbred called the Tchenarani, which has been produced since 1700 by crossing Persian stallions with Turkmene broodmares. This horse is similar in appearance to the Jaf and Darashouri but is distinguishable by its sloping croup and powerful hindquarters.

4 HISPANO

Breed Hispano (Spanish Anglo-Arab).
Place of origin Spain.
Geographical distribution Spain.
Aptitudes Riding horse.
Qualities Good jumper.
Temperament Quiet but energetic.
Conformation A horse with pronounced Arabian features; height at withers 14·3–16 hands (1·50–1·62 m); the coat is usually bay, chestnut or gray. The head is well-proportioned, with a straight profile. The neck is of a good length, the withers high and clearly defined, the back straight, the croup slightly sloping, the tail well set-on, the chest full and deep, and the shoulder long and sloping. The legs are strong with solid joints, prominent tendons, and a tough hoof.
History This horse is the result of crosses between Arab-Spanish mares and English Thoroughbred stallions which explains why the animal has all the features of an Anglo-Arab. Because of its great courage it is sometimes used to test the fighting spirit and stamina of young bulls chosen for the bullring, but being an excellent jumper with a good temperament it is more often used in equestrian sports, its versatility making it equally well-suited for various competitive events from show jumping to dressage.

5 ANDALUSIAN

Breed Andalusian.
Place of origin Spain.
Geographical distribution Europe and South America.
Aptitudes Riding horse.
Qualities Good jumper.
Temperament Balanced and energetic.
Conformation A horse of the mesomorphic type, measuring 15·1–15·3 hands (1·55–1·60 m) at the withers and weighing around 1,250 lb (570 kg). The coat may be gray, bay, black, chestnut or roan. It has a handsome head, with a straight or sometimes convex profile, the ears are small with the tips facing outwards, the large eyes are expressive. The neck is well-proportioned, curved and well set-on, the back straight and short, the quarters rounded, the tail low-set, thick and wavy; the chest is broad and deep with well-curved ribs, the abdomen is roundish, and the shoulder muscular and nicely sloping. The legs are strong with broad joints, the cannons and pasterns long, the hoof well-formed.
History The Andalusian most probably descends from the Barbs and Arabs introduced into Spain during the Moorish invasion of the eighth century A.D., which were crossed time and again with native breeds, especially ponies. According to another theory, however, it is descended from the *Equus ibericus*, which, conversely, contributed to the development of the Barb, having crossed the isthmus that then linked Africa with Europe (the present-day Straits of Gibraltar), thus reaching North Africa. Finally, there are those who claim that the Andalusian is descended from the two thousand Numidian mares that were shipped across the Mediterranean to Spain by the Carthaginian general Hasdrubal.

From the twelfth to the seventeenth century the Andalusian dominated horse breeding in Spain, its only rival being the Arab. Either directly, or through the Neapolitan horse, itself a descendant of the Andalusian, it influenced most European breeds, and as a result of having been shipped across the ocean by Christopher Columbus on his second expedition across the Atlantic, has contributed to the development of almost all American breeds. The most important European breeds to have been influenced are the Lipizzaner, the Frisian, the Hackney, the Kladruber, the Frederiksborg, the Oldenburg, the Holstein, the old Norman horse, and the Orlov; of the American breeds the Quarter Horse and the Criollo have been most markedly influenced. Systematic breeding of the Andalusian began in 1571 when Philip II of Spain founded the royal stables at Cordoba. The horse was greatly admired in the past for its elegant gait which included the *paso de andatura*, a high-stepping movement that is very effective in parades.

The jennet, a small Spanish horse bred in Granada by Berber peoples from the upland regions of Andalusia, and very popular in the Middle Ages, is said to descend from the Andalusian.

The breed commonly known as the Andalusian should more properly be defined as the "Spanish Horse," as the true Andalusian differs in various features: it is of a heavier build, it does not include gray or chestnut in its range of coats, the height at the withers does not exceed 15·1 hands (1.55 m), the back is more gathered, the quarters are more developed and the foot is smaller. Although this breed is not now as popular as it once was, it is still of considerable importance because of its distinctive influence on many modern breeds. Today it is mostly used for pleasure riding, and it is only in the bullring or at the *corrida* that it relives its glorious past.

6 CARTHUSIAN

Breed Carthusian.
Place of origin Spain.
Geographical distribution Spain.
Aptitudes Riding horse, light draft.
Qualities Elegant action, good conformation.
Temperament Docile and quiet.
Conformation A horse of strong, athletic build, approximately 15·2 hands (1·55 m) at the withers; the coat is predominantly gray, but chestnut and black are also found. The head is light and well set-on, the profile slightly convex, with a broad forehead, the ears small, and the eyes large and lively. The neck is correctly proportioned, arched and well set-on, the chest is broad, and the shoulder fairly sloping. The legs are sturdy with broad, clearly defined joints; it has good conformation.
History The breed originated from the studs founded by Carthusian monks in Seville and other parts of Andalusia. These monks, who from 1476 lived in Jérez de la Frontera, devoted themselves to the selective breeding of Andalusian horses, systematically using both the Arab and the Barb in the development of the Carthusian. Today Carthusians are reared in state-owned studs around Cordoba, Jérez de la Frontera and Badajoz. The predominance of the gray coat is attributed to the important influence of two stallions of this color in the first half of the twentieth century. Most of today's Carthusians are descended from the famous stallion Esclavo.
Note Today the Carthusian is rarely categorized into a separate breed and is considered a branch of the Andalusian.

---

7 LUSITANO

Breed Lusitano.
Place of origin Portugal.
Geographical distribution Portugal.
Aptitudes Riding horse, light draft, light farm work.
Qualities Agile, easy to handle, very frugal.
Temperament Docile.
Conformation A horse of the mesomorphic type, standing 15–16 hands (1·52–1·62 m) at the withers; the most usual colors are gray, brown or chestnut. The head is small but with a rather pronounced jaw, the profile straight, the ears small, the eyes lively; the neck is quite thick but well set-on and slightly arched. The withers are clearly visible but not too pronounced, the back is short and straight, the croup rounded, the tail low-set, the chest broad, the shoulder muscular and correctly sloping, the forearm and thigh long, joints solid, and the natural stance good.
History The origins of this horse are uncertain but are probably similar to those of the Andalusian, which it resembles in some respects. Historically it was used for military purposes and as a carriage horse. Today, although it is still used for light farm work, its most important rôle is in Portuguese bullfights, in which the *rejoneador* confronts the bull on horseback. The skill of this *torero* is in avoiding any injury to his mount. Although the Lusitano is the top Portuguese breed, it is now clearly in decline.

8 ALTÉR-REAL

Breed Altér-Real.
Place of origin Portugal.
Aptitudes Riding horse.
Qualities Intelligent, quick to learn.
Temperament Quiet.
Conformation A horse of the meso-dolichomorphic type, standing 15·1–16·1 hands (1·52–1·62 m) at the withers; the coat may be bay, brown, gray or chestnut. The head is of average proportions, with pronounced jaws, a straight or more often slightly convex profile, full forelock, expressive eyes, quite short, muscular neck, arched and with a silky, flowing mane; the withers are pronounced, the back short, the loins powerful, the croup muscular and rounded, the tail well set-on, long and full, the chest broad and deep, and the shoulder muscular and nicely sloping. The legs are solid and well-muscled, the thigh muscular, the cannons and pasterns slender but sturdy, the tendons clean and strong, and the hoof well-formed.
History This breed owes its origins to the three hundred mares selected and imported in 1747 by the House of Braganza, with a view to establishing a national stud at Vila de Portel in the province of Alentejo in southern Portugal. Later in the eighteenth century the Altér-Real was used for the performance of high school exercises in the royal manège. The breed was seriously contaminated at the time of the Napoleonic invasion when Arab, English Thoroughbred, Norman, and Hanoverian blood was introduced. However, as a result of the subsequent introduction of Andalusian horses, which was continued into the twentieth century by government intervention, the breed has been reestablished.

9 FRISIAN

Breed Frisian.
Place of origin Holland.
Aptitudes Draft, farm work, riding horse.
Qualities Excellent trotting horse.
Temperament Docile, responsive.
Conformation A horse of the meso-brachymorphic type with a compact build and superb bearing, standing approximately 15 hands (1·52 m) at the withers. The coat is exclusively black, very rarely presenting white markings on the head only. The head is long and narrow with a straight profile, full forelock, short, pointed ears, and gentle, expressive eyes. The neck is quite short but well-arched; the withers broad and not very prominent, the back straight and short, the loins broad, the flanks rounded, the croup muscular and sloping, the tail full, the chest broad and deep, and the shoulder long and sloping. The legs are muscular with broad joints and some feather below the cannons; the foot is large and strong.
History The Frisian is one of the oldest breeds in Europe and was much in demand in the Middle Ages as a war horse. Although greatly influenced by the addition of Andalusian and Oriental blood, the modern breed still retains the characteristics of its ancestors. An excellent trotter, it was frequently used as a carriage horse. Known at one time as the Harddraver, meaning "good trotter" in Dutch, it has, together with the Hackney, which itself derives from the Frisian, contributed to the formation of all competitive trotting breeds. The Frisian was in danger of becoming extinct in the early twentieth century.

10 DUTCH WARM-BLOOD

Breed Dutch Warm-blood.
Place of origin Holland.
Aptitudes Riding horse, light draft.
Qualities Good jumper.
Temperament Quiet, willing.
Conformation A horse of the meso-dolichomorphic type measuring approximately 16·2 hands (1·62 m) at the withers; the coat may be bay, brown, black, chestnut or gray. The head is well-proportioned, the profile straight or slightly convex, the forehead wide, the ears a nice size and mobile. The neck is a good length, muscular and well set-on; the withers are prominent, the back straight, the loins powerful, the croup slightly sloping, the tail well set-on, the chest broad and deep, and the shoulder long and sloping. The legs are strong and well-muscled, the joints broad and clean, the forearm long, the tendons strong, and the foot well-proportioned, with solid horn.
History This horse derives from two much older Dutch breeds, the Gelderland and the Groningen, with infusions of blood from the English Thoroughbred and stallions from the principle breeds of riding horses in France and Germany. The Stud Book of this breed goes back to 1958 and is held by the Dutch Warm-blood Society. This horse is gifted with a particularly supple, flowing action that adds greatly to its attractive appearance. The Dutch Warm-blood is distinguished in the field of sport, two well-known members of the breed being Calypso, winner of the Volvo World Cup, and Dutch Courage who won the bronze medal at the Dressage World Championships in 1978.

11 GELDERLAND

Breed Gelderland.
Place of origin Holland.
Aptitudes Light draft, riding horse, farm work.
Qualities Good jumper.
Temperament Docile.
Conformation A horse of the mesomorphic type, measuring 15·2–16 hands (1·54–1·63 m) at the withers; the coat is chestnut, bay, black or gray, often with white markings. The head is long and rather flat, the profile straight. The neck is well-proportioned, muscular and arched; the withers fairly prominent and broad merging with the line of the neck; the back is straight and long, the croup short, broad and flat, the tail set high; the chest is full and deep, and the shoulder nicely sloping. The legs are well-muscled, the forearm quite long, and the hoof broad.
History This breed can be traced back to mares native to the Gelderland province, crossed with Andalusian, Neapolitan, Norman, and Norfolk Roadster stallions. In the nineteenth century the breed benefited from the introduction of Anglo-Norman, Oldenburg, and Hackney blood. The Gelderland has an elegant bearing, flowing action, and effective high-stepping trot, suiting it to light draft work and leisure riding. The present trend is to cross this breed with other riding horses, particularly the English Thoroughbred, and the produce has made an important contribution to the development of the Dutch Warm-blood.

Breed English Thoroughbred (Thoroughbred).
Place of origin Great Britain.
Geographical distribution Worldwide.
Aptitudes Flat and jump racing, riding horse.
Qualities Speed, stamina.
Temperament Highly strung, energetic.
Conformation A horse of elegant lines and harmonious form, of the dolichomorphic type. The height at the withers varies from 14·3 to 17 hands (1·50–1·73 m) and the weight from 320 to 450 kg (705 to 990 lb). The coat can be bay, dark bay, black, chestnut and gray; roan and red roan are rarely found. White markings are frequently present both on the head and limbs. The head is small and well set-on, with a straight profile, well-proportioned and mobile ears, large, lively eyes, flared nostrils and thin lips. The neck is long and straight (sometimes slightly arched), well-shaped and well set-on; the withers are prominent and clean, the back long, the loins well set-on to the croup, which may be sloping (in the sprinter) or flat (in the stayer); the tail is set-on high, the chest is high, wide (in the stayer), and deep (in the sprinter), the abdomen tucked up; the shoulder is nicely sloping (straighter in the sprinter), long and well-muscled. The legs are long and well-formed, the joints large and clean, the forelegs are short and muscular, with a long forearm, the thigh and leg are long and muscular, the cannon often thin, the tendons clean, well-defined, and strong, the pasterns are long, the hooves small, well-formed and strong. The skin is very fine, allowing superficial veins to show through.
History The origins of the English Thoroughbred go back to the early eighteenth century and the importation into England of three stallions: the Byerley Turk (a dark bay Arab), the Darley Arabian (an exquisite bay of Arab origin) and the Godolphin Arabian (a brown horse also of Arab origin, although sometimes referred to as a Barb). These three stallions are the foundation sires from whom all modern Throroughbreds can trace their descent in the direct male line, although according to calculations made by Joseph Osborne in 1881, 475 other stallions, all of Oriental origin, contributed in some measure to the breed. Of the one hundred broodmares entered in the Stud Book only forty have kept their direct female line alive through their descendants. These broodmares, initially a small nucleus known as the "Royal Mares," were the result of a closely supervised, selective breeding programme, involving the consistent input of Oriental blood. Three major bloodlines descend directly from the three foundation sires: from the Byerley Turk in the fourth generation, Herod (b. 1758); from the Darley Arabian also in the fourth generation, Eclipse (c. 1764, called in his day "the fleetest horse that ever ran in England"), and from the Godolphin Arabian in the second generation, Matchem (b. 1748, whose maternal grandsire Partner was a grandson of the Byerley Turk).

The English Thoroughbred does not present very uniform morphological features, and can be categorized into three physical types each with different qualities: the "stayer," smaller, and more gathered, with good stamina over distances; the "sprinter," tall, with a long back and loins, very fast; and the "middle-distancer" with a sloping croup, sloping shoulder, and a rather short back, well-suited to steeplechases. The Stud Book dates back to 1791 and is kept up to date by the Jockey Clubs of various countries. The English Jockey Club was founded in 1750.

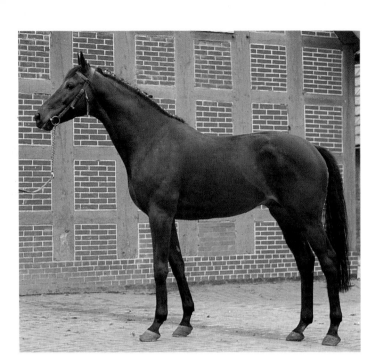

13 CLEVELAND BAY

Breed Cleveland Bay.
Place of origin Great Britain.
Aptitudes Riding horse, light and medium draft, farm work.
Qualities Resistant, longevity.
Temperament Docile.
Conformation A horse of the mesomorphic type standing 16–16·2 hands (1·62–1·65 m) at the withers. The coat may be bay or brown; white marks, other than a very small star, are not admissible. The head is quite large, with a slightly convex profile, large ears, and gentle, expressive eyes. The neck is long and well-muscled, the withers not very pronounced, the back long and straight, the croup long and slightly sloping, the tail set-on; the chest is broad and deep, the shoulder sloping and muscular. The legs are quite short, strong and well-muscled, with broad, clean joints, long cannons but relatively short pasterns; the foot is broad but well-proportioned with tough horn, bluish in color.
History This breed originated during the Middle Ages in the Cleveland district of Yorkshire. It was used by traveling merchants known as "chapmen," hence its nickname, the "Chapman Horse." It shows great versatility in a wide range of tasks. In the second half of the eighteenth century, with the infusion of blood from the English Thoroughbred and the Arab, it became highly prized as a coach horse, a rôle that it has continued to play until the present day, particularly in Britain on royal ceremonial occasions. Crossed with the English Thoroughbred it produces animals with excellent bone and stature, particularly suited to hunting, driving and competitions.

14 HACKNEY

Breed Hackney.
Place of Origin Great Britain.
Geographical distribution Great Britain and the United States.
Aptitudes Harness horse.
Qualities Speed and endurance, longevity.
Temperament Spirited.
Conformation A horse of the mesomorphic type, measuring between 14 and 15·3 hands (1·45–1·57 m) at the withers; the coat is usually bay, brown, black or chestnut, while roan is rare; white markings on the head and limbs are frequent. The head is small and well set-on, with a straight or slightly convex profile, a broad forehead, very pricked-up ears, and large eyes. The neck is long and muscular, slightly arched, the withers are rather low, the back short and straight, the quarters long, the tail well set-on, the chest broad and deep, ribs rounded, the abdomen tucked up, and the shoulder rather flat but powerful, sloping but not long. The legs, not too long, are slender but strong, with solid joints, very long cannons, and a well-formed foot, with tough horn.
History The Hackney is descended from the old Norfolk Roadster, which itself descends from Danish horses introduced into England with the army of King Canute in the eleventh century. These horses were crossed with native and Arab horses, English Thoroughbreds and halfbreds deriving from them, as well as with Dutch and Danish Harddravers. The breed was greatly influenced by the stallion Old Shales (son of the English Thoroughbred Blaze) and two other horses: Gold Farmer and Foxhunter, both sons of Sampson. The Hackney is characterized by its high-stepping trot and far-reaching action.

15 WELSH COB

Breed Welsh Cob.
Place of origin Great Britain (Wales).
Aptitudes Light draft, riding horse.
Qualities Endurance, good jumper.
Temperament Gentle, courageous.
Conformation A horse of the mesomorphic type, occupying Section D of the Welsh Stud Book. It stands 14–15·1 hands (1·45–1·54 m) at the withers. All coats are permitted except piebald and skewbald. The head is small but well-proportioned (of pony type), with a straight profile, small, pointed ears and prominent eyes, set well apart. The neck is long, well-muscled and arched, the withers quite pronounced, the back short, the croup long, broad and rounded, the tail set-on high and carried well, the chest broad and deep, the shoulder sloping and muscular. The legs are short but sturdy and well-muscled, with broad, clean joints, the forearm and shin are long, and the pasterns of a good length and angle; the feet are well-proportioned with a strong hoof; slight feather permitted if silky.
History Descended from the Welsh Mountain pony and, in form, similar to the Welsh pony of Cob type. Although its precise origins are unclear the Hackney, Arab and Spanish Horse may have contributed to its development. Gifted with a particularly splendid action, it was used historically for drawing carriages and has, more recently, become popular in competitive driving. Today it is also used as a riding horse and copes well with difficult terrain, making it ideal for pony trekking, hunting and local show jumping.

16 IRISH HUNTER

Breed Irish Hunter.
Place of origin Ireland.
Geographical distribution Worldwide.
Aptitudes Riding horse.
Qualities Very good jumper, good stamina.
Temperament Quiet and docile.
Comformation A horse of the mesomorphic type, standing 16–17·1 hands (1·62–1·70 m) at the withers; the coat may be bay, brown, black, gray or chestnut. The head is nicely proportioned, with well-delineated jaws, and a straight or slightly convex profile. The neck is long and well-muscled, slightly arched and well set-on; the withers clean and prominent, the back short, the croup broad, muscular and slightly sloping, the chest full and deep, the shoulder sloping and well-muscled. The legs are solid and well-muscled, with broad, clean joints, clearly defined tendons, and a well-formed foot, with tough horn.
History This horse is the issue of a crossing between the English Thoroughbred and the Irish Draft Horse. Consequently, although it is not regarded as a breed in the true sense, but rather as a halfbred, the constancy of its morphological features cause it to be listed among other breeds with a capital letter. Bred for the hunt and suited to all kinds of terrain, because of its sure-footedness, courage and exceptional qualities as a jumper, it is also used for show jumping and eventing. There are three distinct categories depending on the weight of the rider that the horse can support: light (up to 170 lb/75 kg); medium (up to 185 lb/82 kg); heavy (up to 215 lb/95 kg).

17 IRISH COB

Breed Irish cob.
Place of origin Ireland.
Geographical distribution Ireland.
Aptitudes Riding horse, light draft.
Qualities Strong, good jumper.
Conformation A horse of the mesomorphic type, standing 15–15·2 hands (1·53–1·54 m) at the withers; the coat may be bay, brown, black, gray, or chestnut. The head is distinguished, with a convex profile and small ears. The neck is rather short and muscular; the withers are quite pronounced, the back short and straight. The croup is rounded and muscular, the tail well set-on, the chest broad, the shoulder powerful and nicely sloping. The legs are short but sturdy, and the foot rounded with a strong hoof.
History Although it has been bred since the eighteenth century through crosses with the Connemara, the Irish Draft and the English Thoroughbred, the Irish cob cannot be considered an established breed as it does not have stable characteristics and often exceeds the height limits for its category. A cob should stand 14 to 15·5 hands (1·44–1·54 m) at the withers, and have a typically compact and sturdy frame, with short limbs, and a well-developed musculature; the action should be lively and agile. The Irish cob, is generally classed as a type rather than a breed, and was developed with a view to producing energetic horses with good stamina, suitable both for riding and harnessing. Although its use as a working horse has been largely superseded by the advent of motorization, with the increase in popularity of leisure riding, the Irish cob is now used for riding holidays and local shows.

18 FREDERIKSBORG

Breed Frederiksborg.
Place of origin Denmark.
Aptitudes Light draft work, carriage horse, riding horse.
Qualities Agile, strong.
Temperament Docile but lively.
Conformation A horse of the mesomorphic type, standing 15·1–16·1 hands (1·55–1·65 m) at the withers; the coat is always chestnut. The head is well-proportioned, with a straight, or sometimes convex profile, pricked-up ears, and expressive eyes. The neck is well-proportioned, slightly arched, muscular and well set-on; the withers are broad and muscular, but quite pronounced, the back straight, the loins broad, the croup broad and rounded, the tail well set-on, the chest high, full and fairly deep, and the shoulder muscular and nicely sloping. The legs are well-muscled with broad joints, the foot small with tough horn.
History The breed was created in 1562 at the royal stud in Frederiksborg, by King Frederik II of Denmark, using contributions from Neapolitan and Andalusian stallions. It was highly prized as a good school horse because of its reliability and its elegance made it suitable for use as a high-class carriage horse and in military parades. After having contributed to the development of other breeds, including the Lipizzaner and the Orlov Trotter, the Frederiksborg suffered a period of decline in which the continuity of the breed was interrupted. In 1939 it reappeared and was further developed first with the addition of Frisian and Oldenburg blood and later by English Thoroughbred and Arab blood. Today only a small number of representatives of this old breed remain in Denmark.

19 FRENCH TROTTER

Breed French Trotter.
Place of origin France.
Geographical distribution France, Belgium, Italy, Holland, Switzerland, Austria, Denmark, Finland, Spain, Malta.
Aptitudes Racing trotter (in harness and under saddle).
Qualities Speed and endurance.
Temperament Quiet but energetic.
Conformation A sturdy horse of robust and powerful build, of the dolichomorphic type, standing between 15·1 and 16·2 (1·55–1·65 m) at the withers. The most common coats are bay, dark bay, black, chestnut, dark chestnut, and occasionally gray. The head is handsome and well set-on, with a straight profile, broad forehead, long ears, set well apart, lively eyes, and flared nostrils. The neck, well-formed and muscular, is broad at the base and well set-on; the withers are prominent and clean, the back straight, the loins well-developed, the croup long, wide and slightly sloping, the tail set-on quite low, the chest wide and deep, the abdomen drawn up, the shoulder muscular and nicely sloping. The legs are slender but sturdy and muscular, with large, clean joints; the hocks are solid and well-formed, the feet sometimes delicate and better suited to soft ground. The skin is thin and elastic.
History The French Trotter is also known as the Norman Trotter, since its origins are closely interrelated with those of the old Norman horse. Breed selection began in 1836, when the first official speed races for trotters were held on Cherbourg race-course. A determining rôle in the formation of the breed was initially played by the Norfolk (the forerunner of the present-day Hackney), halfbred English hunters, the English Thoroughbred and later the Hackney itself. Later, contributions were also made by the Orlov and the American Trotter (American Standardbred); the latter breed has had lasting influence, in the past through Sam Williams (br. 1922) and the Great McKinney (b. 1922), and more recently through Florestan and Granit, both the progeny of the celebrated Roquépine, but sired respectively by Star's Pride and Ayres, two great American stallions. All trotting breeds have similar, if not actually shared, origins, and inherit their aptitude for trotting from Norfolk horses and from the English Thoroughbred Sampson (1745 out of Blaze); the French Trotter was also particularly influenced by the English Thoroughbred Orville (b. 1799). The foundation sires of the breed were Conquérant (1858), Lavater (1867), Normand (1869), Niger (1869), and Phaëton (1871), from which, by the beginning of the twentieth century, ninety-five per cent of French Trotters were descended. Later, selection was concentrated solely on Conquérant and Phaëton and, to a lesser extent, on Normand. One of Conquérant's descendants is the famous Fuchsia (1883) who, together with Phaëton, has left his distinctive stamp on the breed. However, as with many other racing breeds, the French Trotter lacks uniformity in conformation and general build as a result of the selection criteria, which are oriented towards the perpetuation of functional, rather than aesthetic characteristics.

The French Trotter differs from the American in its greater endurance and slower development, the American breed being decidedly more precocious. It is also used in mounted trotting races. The speed record for the breed is currently held by Minou du Donjon, and was established in Stockholm in 1985 with a kilometer time of 1′11⁵⁄₁₀″. The Stud Book was begun in 1922, and membership has been strictly controlled since 1941.

Breed French Anglo-Arab.
Place of origin France.
Geographical distribution Europe.
Aptitudes Riding horse.
Qualities Excellent competition horse.
Temperament Quiet but energetic.
Conformation A horse of the dolichomorphic type, standing 15·2–16·3 hands (1·55–1·67 m) at the withers. The most usual colors are bay and chestnut, while gray is more rare. It has a small head, well set-on, with a straight or concave profile, broad forehead, small ears, and large eyes. The neck is well-proportioned, muscular and well set-on; the withers are high and well-defined, the back straight, the loins short and broad, the croup long and flat, the tail well set-on, the chest wide and deep, the shoulder long and sloping. The legs are robust and strong, with clean joints and clearly defined tendons, the forearm and shin are long and well-muscled, the foot solid, the natural stance good. The skin is thin.
History After various earlier attempts had met with little success, in around 1843 the veterinarian E. Gayot determined to create an Anglo-Arab breed, first at the Le Pin, and subsequently at the Pompadour stud farms. He was so successful in his attempt that he is now regarded as the father of the French Anglo-Arab breed. However, others before him had opened the way with work undertaken at the stud farms at Tarbes and Pau in southwest France, originally founded by Napoleon. The breed developed from a nucleus of broodmares of Oriental origin that were probably descended from horses abandoned by the Moors, in retreat after the Battle of Poitiers in 732 A.D., during their flight southward over the Pyrenees. These horses interbred with local horse populations to produce the Tarbes and Limousin breeds, from which, with the addition of other Arab and English Thoroughbred blood, the French Anglo-Arab would seem to originate. The modern French Anglo-Arab descends from the Arab stallion Massoud (1814–1843) and the Turkish stallion Aslan, imported into France from Egypt, and three English Thoroughbred broodmares: Selim Mare, Comus Mare and Daer, all of which greatly influenced the breed. Another stallion to have a decisive influence in fixing the characteristics of the breed was Prisme (1890–1917).

The French Anglo-Arab is a solidly built horse, with good conformation and a distinguished bearing, and is today regarded as one of the best riding breeds in the world. An absolute requirement for registration in the Stud Book is the presence of at least twenty-five per cent Arab blood and the absence in the pedigree of horses of other breeds for at least the last six generations. Since 1976 horses with less than twenty-five per cent Arab blood are known as "F.A.A." or "Facteur d'Anglo-Arab" as it is possible to obtain a horse meeting the requirements for registration from a mare with less than the minimum level of Arab blood by mating it back with a purebred Arab, or with an Anglo-Arab with a high percentage of Arab blood. This dinstinction is not made in Britain. The breed Stud Book is represented by the first section of the Livre généalogique des chevaux français, maintained by the Service des Haras nationaux et de l'Équitation.

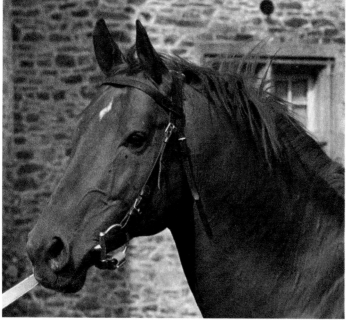

21 SELLE FRANÇAIS

Breed Selle Français.
Place of origin France.
Geographical distribution Europe.
Aptitudes Riding horse.
Qualities Good competition horse.
Temperament Quiet but energetic.
Conformation A horse of the meso-dolichomorphic type, measuring 15·1–17 hands (1·55–1·75 m) at the withers. There are five different types of Selle Français; three of medium weight and two of the heavy type. In the medium-weight category there is the small type (up to 15·1 hands/1·55 m), the medium type (15·1–16 hands/1·55–1·63 m) and the large type (over 16 hands/1·63 m). The heavy type is subdivided into small (up to 16 hands/1·63 m) and large (over 16 hands/1·63 m). The distinction between the medium-weight and heavy-weight categories lies in the horse's ability to carry riders of different weights. The most usual colors of coat are chestnut, bay and brown; gray and red roan are more rare. The head is small and well set-on, with pronounced jaws, a straight or convex profile, long ears and deep-set eyes. The neck is long, well-muscled and well set-on; the withers are long and prominent, the back straight, the croup long, muscular and slightly sloping, the chest broad and deep, the shoulder long and nicely sloping. The legs are solid and well-muscled with clean joints, short, slender cannons, and clearly defined tendons. The foot has tough horn.
History This horse is the natural descendant of the ancient Norman breed. At the end of the eighteenth century the precise origins of the horse population in Normandy were unclear although they were undoubtedly influenced by Arab horses introduced into France at the time of the Crusades. The basic stock was further influenced by Young Rattler (1811), a direct import from England. Sired by the English Thoroughbred Rattler and out of the daughter of another English Thoroughbred, Snap, Young Rattler is regarded as the foundation sire of the Norman breed, also giving rise to Normand, one of the foundation sires of the French Trotter.

Today the Norman horse no longer exists, and has been superseded by the Selle Français. It has, however, been survived by its cob version, a horse of the mesomorphic or meso-brachymorphic type, well-suited to farm work, weighing between 1,200 and 1,760 lb (550–800 kg) and measuring between 15·3 and 16·3 hands (1·6–1·70 m).

The Stud Book for the Selle Français was established in 1950 and admits selected, but not necessarily purebred, mares, and English Thoroughbred, Arab, Anglo-Arab, and French Trotter stallions, all of which breeds have contributed to the development of the present-day type. Of the animals belonging to this relatively new breed, forty-five per cent were sired by a Selle Français, thirty-three per cent by an English Thoroughbred, twenty per cent by an Arab and two per cent by a French Trotter. Also admitted are crosses between English Thoroughbreds and French Trotters, and between Arabs or Anglo-Arabs and French Trotters.

22 SWISS WARM-BLOOD

Breed Swiss Warm-blood.
Place of origin Switzerland.
Aptitudes Riding horse, light draft.
Qualities Good competition horse.
Temperament Docile.
Conformation A horse of the meso-dolichomorphic type, measuring 15·1–16·2 hands (1·55–1·64 m) at the withers; the coat can be any color. The head is well-proportioned, with a straight or slightly convex profile. The neck is a good length and well set-on; the withers are prominent, the back straight, the croup slightly sloping, the tail well set-on, the chest broad and deep, and the shoulder long and sloping. The legs are strong with good joints and well-defined tendons, the foot is well-formed with strong horn.
History The main Swiss foundation stock is the Einsiedler, a breed that originated in Einsiedeln in the Swiss canton of Schwyz. Here, in a Benedictine monastery there is evidence of the existence of a stud dating back to 1064. Like many breeds, the Einsiedler was developed by monks, having in time been modified by the introduction of the Hackney and the Norman. During the twentieth century French blood was systematically introduced and in the nineteen-sixties Thoroughbred, Swedish and German blood was added to start the Swiss Warm-blood. At first the stallions were mainly imports, but today at the National Stud of Avenches more and more Swiss Warm-bloods are being used to produce this talented competition horse.

23 MAREMMANA

Breed Maremmana.
Place of origin Italy (Latium and Tuscany).
Aptitudes Riding horse, light draft, farm work.
Qualities Hardy, frugal, resistant, good jumper.
Temperament Well-balanced, energetic, enduring.
Conformation A horse of the meso-dolichomorphic type, solidly built, measuring between 15–15·3 hands (1·55–1·60 m) at the withers; the coat is usually bay, brown, burnt chestnut or black; rarely gray or roan. The head is long and slightly heavy, with a ewe-like profile. The neck is a good length and muscular, quite broad at the base; withers high and well-muscled, the back short and straight, the loins short, the croup sloping, the chest full, and the shoulder nicely sloping. The legs are solid and sturdy, with good joints and correct natural stance; the hoof is well-shaped and proportioned, with strong horn.
History Reared in the wild state this horse is the classic mount of the *butteri* or cattlemen in the Maremma region of Tuscany and Latium. It is a solidly built animal, able to withstand bad weather conditions and to adapt to every type of terrain, however awkward. In recent times it has been crossed with the English Thoroughbred: the result has been an increase in stature and a more refined appearance, but at the expense of the hardiness and exceptional stamina that characterized the classic Maremmana. This modern breed which is known as the "improved" Maremmana is developing more as a dolichomorphic type. In the Italian province of Pesaro a breed known as the Catria Horse is reared, which has been obtained by crossing the Maremmana with Franches-Montagnes stallions.

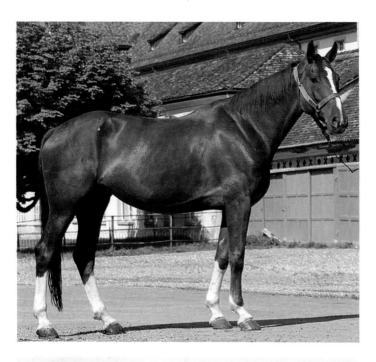

24 MURGESE

Breed Murgese.
Place of origin Italy (Apulia).
Aptitudes Farm work, light draft, riding horse.
Qualities Hardy.
Temperament Docile but lively.
Conformation A horse of the mesomorphic type, standing 14–15 hands (1·45–1·55 m) at the withers; the coat may be black, gray with a black head, or brown. The head is light, sometimes with a prominent jawline, a straight or slightly ewe-like profile, broad forehead, and small ears. The neck is sturdy, broad at the base with a full mane; the withers quite pronounced, the back straight but occasionally slightly hollow, the loins broad and short, the croup long and broad, tending to be flat or sloping, the chest is full and well-developed, and the shoulder nicely sloping. The legs are strong with large joints, the forearm of medium length, the thigh of a good length, the cannons and pasterns short, and the hoof regular and hard; good natural stance.
History The origins of this breed date back to the time of Spanish rule in Italy. Its early development was influenced by both Barb and Arab stallions imported by the Count of Conversano: this dual influence can be seen in the alternating character of certain features, such as the croup, which may be flat as in the Arab, or sloping as in the Barb. Selection of the present-day Murgese began in 1926, and the horses are reared in the wild state in a harsh environment of scrubby grazing land with oak and mixed woodland in hilly areas. Because of its hardy nature the horse is used for trekking and cross-country riding.

---

25 SARDINIAN ANGLO-ARAB

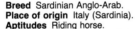

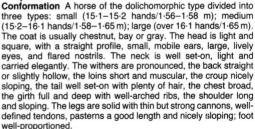

Breed Sardinian Anglo-Arab.
Place of origin Italy (Sardinia).
Aptitudes Riding horse.
Qualities Hardy, swift, good staying power, good jumper.
Temperament Well-balanced.
Conformation A horse of the dolichomorphic type divided into three types: small (15·1–15·2 hands/1·56–1·58 m); medium (15·2–16·1 hands/1·58–1·65 m); large (over 16·1 hands/1·65 m). The coat is usually chestnut, bay or gray. The head is light and square, with a straight profile, small, mobile ears, large, lively eyes, and flared nostrils. The neck is well set-on, light and carried elegantly. The withers are pronounced, the back straight or slightly hollow, the loins short and muscular, the croup nicely sloping, the tail well set-on with plenty of hair, the chest broad, the girth full and deep with well-arched ribs, the shoulder long and sloping. The legs are solid with thin but strong cannons, well-defined tendons, pasterns a good length and nicely sloping; foot well-proportioned.
History From the time when the Saracens dominated Sardinia Arab horses were crossed with native breeds of smaller stature. In the early sixteenth century Ferdinand V, known as "the Catholic," imported Andalusian stallions to improve the breed. The breed went into a decline at the beginning of the eighteenth century but, as a result of the input of new Arab blood at the start of the twentieth century it was revived. More recently the Arab has been substituted by the English Thoroughbred, and this has led to the formation of the Sardinian Anglo-Arab of today, very different in size and structure from its forefathers.

26 SALERNO

Breed Salerno (Persano).
Place of origin Italy (Campania).
Aptitudes Riding horse.
Qualities Good jumper.
Temperament Quiet, balanced, energetic.
Conformation A horse of the meso-dolichomorphic type, standing 16·1–17 hands (1·62–1·70 m) at the withers; the coat is bay, chestnut, black or gray. The head is light and well set-on, with a straight profile, wide, square forehead, lively eyes, and flared nostrils. The neck is long and well set-on; the withers quite pronounced and muscular, the back well-proportioned, the loins short, the croup muscular and rounded, the girth deep, and the shoulder long and nicely sloping. The cannons are slender but strong, tendons well-defined and clean, the hoof has strong horn.
History The Salerno descends from the Neapolitan, a breed that was popular in the Middle Ages, with important infusions of Spanish and Oriental blood. During the Bourbon period Charles III, king of Naples, promoted this horse from 1783 onward. With the unification of Italy the breeding program suffered greatly and was finally suppressed in 1874, however, at the beginning of the twentieth century the breed was slowly and carefully restored, first as a valuable carriage horse and then later as a superb riding horse. Its riding qualities were improved by the systematic use in breeding of English Thoroughbred stallions, rather than Arabs, which had been used in the past, placing particular emphasis on animals with good staying power. The result of this change in breeding policy has been an increase in the size and almost total disappearance of the once common gray coat.

27 CALABRESE

Breed Calabrese.
Place of origin Italy (Calabria).
Aptitudes Riding horse.
Qualities Dependable, tireless.
Temperament Active, lively, docile.
Conformation A horse of the meso-dolichomorphic type, measuring 16–16·2 hands (1·60–1·65 m) at the withers; the coat is usually bay, brown, black, gray or chestnut. It has a well-formed head, with a straight or slightly convex profile. The neck is correctly proportioned; the withers are prominent, the back straight, the loins short, the croup slanting, the chest broad and deep, the shoulder long and sloping. The tendons are strong, the hoof well-formed with strong horn; good natural stance.
History Originally of Arab derivation, this horse was crossed during the Bourbon period with the Andalusian from which it inherited a certain elegance of movement. The Calabrese shows remarkable harmony of form and is hardy and dependable, qualities that derive from its Arab blood. More recently the use of English Thoroughbred stallions has both improved its performance and increased its general stature. However, in order to ensure the perpetuation of the breed's distinctive characteristics, Oriental blood is reintroduced from time to time.

28 SICILIAN

Breed Sicilian.
Place of origin Italy (Sicily).
Geographical distribution Italy (Sicily).
Aptitudes Riding horse, light draft.
Qualities Resistance to fatigue, good stamina.
Temperament Spirited, highly strung.
Conformation A horse of the dolichomorphic type, standing 14·3–15·2 hands (1·50–1·55 m) at the withers; the coat is bay, black, chestnut or gray (dappled). The head is light, with a straight or slightly convex profile, small ears, lively eyes, and flared nostrils. The neck is of a good length, muscular and well set-on; withers high, back short, back and loins strong, the croup angular and quite flat, tail well set-on and flowing, the chest broad and deep, the shoulder sloping. The legs are long and muscular with broad, clean joints, strong, well-defined tendons; hoof well-formed and in proportion.
History Rather than a breed as such, the Sicilian is an equine population of clear Anglo-Arab derivation, forming two distinct ethnic groups. Those from the eastern provinces of Sicily (Catania, Syracuse, and Ragusa) are more elegant in appearance with more pronounced dolichomorphic features, while those further inland are more compact and closer to the mesomorphic type, although there is much variation.

29 SAN FRATELLO

Breed San Fratello.
Place of origin Italy (Sicily).
Aptitudes Riding horse, pack horse, light draft.
Qualities Hardy, frugal.
Temperament Lively.
Conformation A horse of the meso-dolichomorphic type with appreciable aesthetic qualities, standing 15–16 hands (1·52–1·58 m) at the withers and weighing 1,100–1,300 lb (500–580 kg). The coat is always black, bay or brown. The head is slightly heavy, with a straight or slightly convex profile, straight ears, and expressive eyes. The neck is correctly proportioned; the withers are quite prominent, the back straight, loins short and strong, flank well-formed, croup wide and muscular, slightly sloping, the tail well set-on, the chest wide and deep, and the shoulder nicely sloping. The legs are nicely shaped and well-muscled, with strong joints and tendons, nicely sloping pasterns, and a strong, well-formed hoof.
History Reared in the wild in Sicily, in the oak and beech woods of the Nebrodi mountains in the province of Messina, the San Fratello is a strong and powerful breed with outstanding resistance. Although it has profited in the past from infusions of Spanish Anglo-Arab, Anglo-Arab, Salerno and, recently, Nonius blood, it has resisted all attempts at improvement, the only other breed it in any way resembles being the Maremmana. Breeding stock is carefully selected, and the colts are trained as pack horses at thirty months. Docile and strong, they are well-suited for trekking holidays and as riding horses.

30 OLDENBURG

Breed Oldenburg.
Place of origin West Germany.
Aptitudes Riding horse, light draft.
Qualities Good jumper, early developer, long-lived.
Temperament Calm but energetic.
Conformation A horse of the meso-dolichomorphic type, standing 16·1–17·1 hands (1·62–1·67 m) at the withers; the coat is usually bay, brown, black or gray, rarely chestnut. The head is of average size, with a straight or convex profile, very pricked-up ears, and flared nostrils. The neck, of average size and muscular, is well set-on and elegantly carried; the withers are quite pronounced, the back straight, the croup broad, flat and well-muscled, the tail is set-on high, the chest is wide and deep, and the shoulder sloping and muscular. The legs are well-muscled, with broad joints, clearly defined tendons and strong hooves.
History The breed derives from the East Frisian, with blood from Spanish, Neapolitan, Anglo-Arab and English Thoroughbred stallions, followed by an important contribution toward the end of the nineteenth century, from the Cleveland Bay. Count Anton Gunther (1603–1667) was the first serious breeder, however, it took almost three centuries to develop the excellent carriage horse of the early twentieth century. To adapt the breed to changing modern requirements, the Oldenburg has been crossed with Hanoverian, Anglo-Norman and English Thoroughbred stallions, producing an all-purpose riding and competition horse.

---

31 TRAKEHNER

Breed Trakehner (East Prussian).
Place of origin West Germany.
Aptitudes Riding horse, light draft.
Qualities Good competition horse, remarkable stamina.
Temperament Quiet but dynamic.
Conformation A horse of the meso-dolichomorphic type, standing 16–16·2 hands (1·62–1·67 m) at the withers; the coat is usually chestnut, bay, brown, black or, more rarely, gray. The head is well-proportioned, with a straight profile and lively eyes. The neck is well-formed, long and well set-on; the withers are quite pronounced, the back straight, the croup slightly sloping, the tail well set-on, the chest deep, and the shoulder well-muscled, long and sloping. The legs are well-muscled, with broad, clean joints, clearly defined tendons, and a solid hoof.
History This breed was created at the Stud of Trakehnen, founded in Lithuania in 1732 by Frederick William I of Prussia for military purposes. Its development was particularly influenced by the "Schweiken," an old local breed that had received infusions of Oriental blood in as far back as the sixteenth century. As a result of a series of crosses, with subsequent contributions from the Arab and the English Thoroughbred, its present-day characteristics were established. At the end of World War II over a thousand horses were taken to West Germany by local inhabitants fleeing from the advancing Russians, and here the stud farms were reconstructed. The horses that remained in East Prussia became known as the Masuren, which was amalgamated with the Poznan to establish the Wielkopolski.

32 HANOVERIAN

Breed Hanoverian.
Place of origin West Germany (Hanover, Lower Saxony).
Geographical distribution Europe, United States.
Aptitudes Riding horse, light draft.
Qualities Good competition horse.
Temperament Courageous and quiet.
Conformation A horse of the meso-dolichomorphic type, standing 15·2–17 hands (1·56–1·72 m) at the withers, and weighing 1,100–1,300 lb (500–600 kg). The coat is usually chestnut, bay, brown, black or gray; white markings are frequent. The head is well-proportioned and well set-on, with well-defined jaws, and a straight or convex profile. The neck is long, well-conformed, and well set-on; the withers are pronounced, the back long and straight, the croup quite long, wide and rounded, the tail well set-on and carried with elegance, the chest wide and deep, and the shoulder long and sloping. The legs are strong and well-muscled, with broad, clean joints, clearly defined tendons and a tough hoof.
History This is a very old breed, which during its development from the early eighteenth century to the present day has greatly altered in physical build and appearance. This process began at about the same time as the accession to the English throne in 1714 of George Louis, Elector of Hanover, who reigned as King George I of England. As a result of this new link between England and Germany, English Thoroughbred blood was introduced into the breed, which, until this time, had only been suited to draft and farm work, owing to its heavy build. In 1735, continuing the work of improving the breed, George II founded a stud farm in the small town of Celle, about 25 miles (40 km) from Hanover, where he succeeded in obtaining a lighter version of the breed. This excellent coach horse was used in Britain for drawing royal carriages until the reign of George V. Toward the end of the nineteenth century the input of English blood was stopped to avoid further modification to the breed that might lessen its suitability for its by now established use. However, with the advent of motorization in agriculture and in general transport the Hanoverian was forced to adapt to new requirements, and new blood was once again introduced, using English Thoroughbred, Arab and also Trakehner blood. A decisive contribution to the Hanoverian's transformation from carriage to all-round competition horse was made by the Trakehner stallion Semper Idem.

The modern Hanoverian is a solid, well-built horse, with good conformation, frequently used to improve other breeds. It is a quiet, courageous animal with remarkable stamina and displays great versatility, performing well in a wide range of sporting activities such as fox hunting, show jumping, dressage, and three-day events.

33 HOLSTEIN

Breed Holstein.
Place of origin West Germany
Aptitudes Riding horse.
Qualities Good competition horse.
Temperament Docile and quiet, but energetic.
Conformation A horse of the meso-dolichomorphic type, standing 16–17 hands (1·62–1·72 m) at the withers. The coat is generally bay, brown, black, gray or chestnut. The head is long, with a straight or slightly convex profile, rather long ears, lively and expressive eyes, and flared nostrils. The neck is long, well-conformed, muscular and carried with elegance; the withers are prominent, the back straight and often long, the back and loins are powerful, the croup broad, muscular, and slightly sloping, the tail well set-on, the chest wide and deep, and the shoulder long, muscular, and sloping. The legs are well-muscled, with broad, clean joints, fairly long cannons, clearly defined tendons, and a tough hoof.
History The Holstein was first bred in the early fourteenth century at stables belonging to the monastery of Uetersen, which lies in the marshlands northeast of the Elbe estuary. During the Middle Ages it was a rather heavy-looking war horse of the same type as the Great Horse. It retained its importance for the military in later periods too, when it was used both as a cavalry horse and as a gun horse for drawing artillery. Contributions to the development of the Holstein have been made over the centuries firstly by Oriental, Spanish and Neapolitan horses, and later by the English Thoroughbred, the Cleveland Bay, and the Trakehner. Since World War II more English Thoroughbred blood has been introduced to produce an excellent competition horse.

34 WÜRTTEMBERG

Breed Württemberg.
Place of origin West Germany.
Geographical distribution West Germany.
Aptitudes Riding horse, light draft, farm work.
Qualities Strong and hardy.
Temperament Steady and docile.
Conformation A horse of the meso-dolichomorphic type, standing about 16·1 hands (1·62 m) at the withers; the coat is generally bay, brown, black or chestnut, with possible white markings. The head is of average size, with a straight profile and very pricked-up ears. The neck is well-conformed and of a good length; the withers are prominent, the back long and straight, the croup slightly sloping, the tail well set-on, the chest deep, the shoulder well-muscled and nicely sloping. The legs are well-muscled, with strong cannons, and tough, well-formed hooves.
History The foundation stock – the Württemberg – can be traced back to the sixteenth century, and was formed at the stud farm of Marbach by crossing native mares with Arab, Caucasian and Suffolk Punch stallions. Subsequent contributions were made by the Trakehner, the Norman and the Anglo-Norman but since the last war it has been the Trakehner that has been used most to refine the breed and turn it into a popular horse for sports. The Württemberg was in the past used for farm work in its native region, while today, the Baden-Württemberg is considered a good riding horse well suited to recreational riding.
Note Germany has other regional breeds, such as the Westphalian, Bavarian, Hessen, Rhineland, Rhineland-Pfalz, and Saar, all of which are based on local stock.

35 EAST FRISIAN

Breed East Frisian.
Place of origin East Germany (Thuringia).
Geographical distribution East Germany.
Aptitudes Riding horse and light draft.
Qualities Elegant movement.
Temperament Lively and courageous.
Conformation A horse of the meso-dolichomorphic type, standing 15·2–16·1 hands (1·54–1·64 m) at the withers; the coat may be bay, brown, black, gray or chestnut. The head is well-proportioned, with a straight profile, lively eyes, and flared nostrils. The neck is long and slightly arched; the withers are quite prominent, the back long and straight, the croup slightly sloping, the tail well set-on, the chest wide and deep, and the shoulder long and nicely sloping. The legs have broad, clean joints, the thigh is muscular, as are the forearm and shin, the tendons are well-defined and strong.
History Until World War II the East Frisian developed in tandem with the Oldenburg, which had similar origins, and crosses and exchanges between the two breeds were frequent. However, the political division of Germany at the end of the war has meant that the two breeds have continued to develop along different lines: the East Frisian has benefited from the use of Arab stallions from the Marbach stud and from the Balbolna stud, in Hungary, the influence of the gray, Gazal, being particularly significant. As a result of this breeding policy, the breed became more refined. More recently, in response to modern demands oriented to the production of all-round sporting horses Hanoverian blood has been introduced.

36 MECKLENBURG

Breed Mecklenburg.
Place of origin East Germany.
Geographical distribution East Germany.
Aptitudes Riding horse.
Qualities Strong and courageous.
Temperament Docile and quiet.
Conformation A horse of the meso-dolichomorphic type, standing 15·3–16 hands (1·54–1·65 m) at the withers; the coat is usually bay, brown, black or chestnut. The head is average size, with a straight profile. The neck is strong and quite long; the withers are prominent, the back straight, the loins broad and powerful, the croup sloping, the chest wide and deep, and the shoulder nicely sloping. The legs are sturdy, with good bone structure and clean joints, the hoof is rounded and hard.
History Once prized as a carriage horse, above all for its remarkable size, this horse, in common with similar breeds, had to undergo a process of transformation in order to survive. Although smaller in build, the present-day Mecklenburg has many features in common with the Hanoverian. After World War II the breed was revived in East Germany, where the stallions are directly controlled by the State; mares generally belong to individual breeders.

37 LIPIZZANER

Breed Lipizzaner.
Place of origin Austria.
Geographical distribution Austria, Yugoslavia, Italy, Hungary.
Aptitudes Riding horse, harness, draft, farm work.
Qualities Frugal, good endurance, willing and intelligent.
Conformation A horse of the meso-dolichomorphic type, standing 15–16·1 hands (1·52–1·65 m) at the withers. The coat is most frequently gray, but may also be bay, black, roan or white. The head is long, with a straight or slightly convex profile, rather pronounced jaws, small ears, large, expressive eyes and flared nostrils. The neck is sturdy, arched and well set-on, the mane full and silky; the withers are not very prominent, broad and muscular, the back long and occasionally slightly hollow, the loins broad and muscular, the croup short, broad and rounded, the tail, well set-on and carried high, is full and formed of long, fine hair, the chest wide and deep, the shoulder sloping and muscular. The legs, strong and hard, are well-muscled, with broad clean joints, well-defined tendons, and the feet small with strong horn, the natural stance is correct.
History The breed takes its name from the village of Lipizza near the northeast Italian border. Although now in Yugoslavia, Lipizza belonged to Italy prior to World War I, and, even earlier, when the breed was being developed, it lay within Austrian territory. For this reason Austria is now considered the birthplace of the breed. The origins of the breed go back to the sixteenth century, its creation being attributed to Archduke Charles of Styria, who began breeding with a nucleus of Italian broodmares imported from Verona, the Po Valley and Aquileia, and two Andalusian stallions brought north from Spain. The breed soon became famous, not least because it supplied horses to the Spanish Riding School in Vienna, founded in 1729 by Charles VI and called "Spanish" to emphasize the high percentage of Andalusian blood in the horses used there. From 1717 onward the Spanish stallions were substituted by Neopolitan, Kladruber and Frederiksborg stallions, which in their turn were superseded by Arab stallions. With the fall of the Austro-Hungarian Empire the stud was transferred to Piber, from where it was evacuated at the end of World War II by the Americans, afraid that the horses might end up in the hands of the Soviets, who were advancing from the east. Today, the Lipizzaner is again reared in Piber (Austria), in Lipizza (Yugoslavia), at Monterotondo (Italy) and at Babolna (Hungary. The Lipizzaner breed may be subdivided into six distinct families descending from six different stallions: two Andalusian (the gray Maestoso and the red roan Favory), two Neapolitan (the brown Conversano and the bay Napolitano), one Frederiksborg (the gray Pluto), and one Arab (the gray Siglavy). The predominance of gray coats among these progenitors accounts for the large incidence of this color in their descendants. It should be noted that gray animals are born black and only acquire their permanent coat as they grow older. The Lipizzaner is a sturdy and long-lived horse, but does not develop early. Its general appearance is harmonious and well-structured, retaining the clear imprint of the Andalusian and the Neapolitan, which is itself derived from the Andalusian.

38 KLADRUBER

Breed Kladruber.
Place of origin Czechoslovakia (Bohemia).
Aptitudes Light draft, heavy draft, riding horse.
Qualities Strong and generous, long-lived.
Temperament Calm but lively.
Conformation A horse of the mesomorphic type, standing 16·2–17 hands (1·63–1·77 m) at the withers; black or gray in color. The head is long, with pronounced jaws, a convex profile, a broad forehead, large eyes, and flared nostrils. The neck is well-proportioned, muscular and slightly arched; the withers are broad and not very prominent, the back long and straight, the loins full, the croup short, wide and rounded, the tail well set-on, flowing and fine, the chest wide and deep, and the shoulder well-muscled and nicely sloping. The legs are strong, with broad, clean joints; the forearm and shin are long, the cannons slender but solid, the tendons strong and clearly defined, the pasterns a little long, and the foot well-formed.
History Created in the sixteenth century at the royal stud of Kladrub in Bohemia, this breed has been very strictly bred, the only outside blood to be used in its formation coming from Neapolitan and Andalusian stallions. The characteristic colors derive from the two foundation sires of the breed: the gray Pepoli (1764) and the black Sacromoso (1799). In the past it was taller in stature than today, sometimes reaching a height of over 18 hands (1·80 m). Four distinct bloodlines can now be distinguished, descending from the stallions Generale, Generalissimus, Sacromoso and Favory. Favory is also the foundation sire of some present-day families of the Lipizzaner.

39 SWEDISH WARM-BLOOD

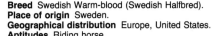

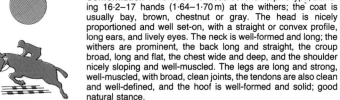

Breed Swedish Warm-blood (Swedish Halfbred).
Place of origin Sweden.
Geographical distribution Europe, United States.
Aptitudes Riding horse.
Qualities Good competition horse.
Temperament Quiet and intelligent.
Conformation A horse of the meso-dolichomorphic type, standing 16·2–17 hands (1·64–1·70 m) at the withers; the coat is usually bay, brown, chestnut or gray. The head is nicely proportioned and well set-on, with a straight or convex profile, long ears, and lively eyes. The neck is well-formed and long; the withers are prominent, the back long and straight, the croup broad, long and flat, the chest wide and deep, and the shoulder nicely sloping and well-muscled. The legs are long and strong, well-muscled, with broad, clean joints, the tendons are also clean and well-defined, and the hoof is well-formed and solid; good natural stance.
History The breed goes back to the early seventeenth century and is derived from native horses subjected to repeated crossing with a variety of very different breeds, such as the Arab, the Andalusian, the Frisian, the Hanoverian, the Trakehner, and the English Thoroughbred. Once used for military purposes, it is today essentially a riding horse much used in sporting competition: a good jumper gifted with particular aptitude for dressage; it is an excellent horse for horse trials.

40 FINNISH UNIVERSAL

Breed Finnish Universal.
Place of origin Finland.
Geographical distribution Finland.
Aptitudes Light draft, trotting races, farm work, riding horse.
Qualities Willing and hard working.
Temperament Docile and good-natured.
Conformation A horse of the mesomorphic type, standing between 14·3 and 15·2 hands (1·50–1·57 m) at the withers and weighing between 1,100 and 1,280 lb (500–580 kg). The coat is generally chestnut, bay, or gray, more rarely brown or black. The head is fairly small but rather heavy and square, with a straight profile, small, pointed ears, and gentle eyes. The neck is strong, of average length, but not well set-on; the withers are quite pronounced, the back rather short, the croup sloping, the tail set-on low, the chest high and deep, the abdomen drawn in, and the shoulder muscular and fairly sloping. The legs are not long, but sturdy, with broad, clean joints, short pasterns, and well-shaped feet.
History The breed is derived from native ponies, crossed with other breeds of varying type and origin. In the past it was bred in two distinct versions: one heavy, for use in more arduous work, the other lighter, similar to the present-day type. A versatile animal, and for this reason described as "Universal," the Finnish horse is also used in harnessed trotting contests, which are very popular throughout Scandinavia.

41 GIDRAN ARABIAN

Breed Gidran (Hungarian Anglo-Arabian).
Place of origin Hungary.
Geographical distribution Hungary, Poland, Bulgaria.
Aptitudes Riding horse and light draft.
Qualities Good jumper.
Temperament Lively and not always docile.
Conformation A horse of the dolichomorphic type, standing 16·1–17 hands (1·60–1·70 m) at the withers; the coat is chestnut. The head is small and well set-on, with a straight profile, small ears, and large, lively eyes. The neck is quite long and well-formed; the withers are prominent, the back straight and long, the croup well-muscled, broad and generally short, the tail well set-on, the chest wide and deep, the shoulder sloping and well-muscled. The legs have strong, well-muscled thighs, rather short cannons, clean, well-defined tendons, and well-formed feet with tough horn; good natural stance.
History The breed was formed in the course of the nineteenth century and takes its name from the stallion Gidran, an Arab of the Siglavy strain, bred at the Babolna stud in Hungary and the son of a stallion of the same name that had been imported from the Middle East in 1816. The characteristics of the present-day breed are the result of repeated crosses with the English Thoroughbred, and it is for this reason that it is known under the name of Hungarian Anglo-Arab. This fiery animal bears great distinction and the stallions are exported to all eastern European countries, for crossing with local mares. Its great jumping skills make the Gidran well-suited to competition events.

42 SHAGYA ARABIAN

Breed Shagya Arabian.
Place of origin Hungary.
Geographical distribution Austria, Germany, Romania, Czechoslovakia, Poland, Yugoslavia, United States.
Aptitudes Riding horse and light draft.
Qualities Speed and stamina.
Temperament Energetic and lively.
Conformation A horse of the mesomorphic type, standing 14·2–15·2 hands (1·48–1·57 m) at the withers; the coat is generally gray in color or, more rarely, black. Its features, particularly in the head, are essentially Arab, the only difference being that the Shagya-Arabian has a larger build.
History The breed was formed at the Babolna stud farms, founded in 1789. There, in 1816, under order from the military authorities, it was decreed that all the broodmares should be crossed with Oriental stallions. A later infusion of Arab blood is recorded between 1830 and 1840, following the importation of stallions and mares direct from the Middle East. Of these stallions, one in particular, a gray, Shagya, was to prove a great breeding stallion, giving rise to a homogeneous line of descendants, almost all of which have his coat.

43 NONIUS

Breed Nonius.
Place of origin Hungary.
Aptitudes Riding horse, light draft, and medium draft.
Qualities Strong and hardy.
Temperament Quiet and docile, but lively.
Conformation A horse of the mesomorphic type, bred in two versions of different statures, the smaller type, standing 14·2–15·2 hands (1·45–1·55 m) at the withers, and the large at 15·2–16·2 hands (1·55–1·65 m). The coat is bay or brown. The head is a little long, but light and well set-on, with a straight or slightly convex profile, a broad forehead, long ears, and flared nostrils. The neck is long and muscular, well set-on; the withers are clean and fairly prominent, the back long but sometimes slightly hollow, the croup rounded but not very broad, the tail well set-on, the chest wide and deep, and the shoulder long and nicely sloping. The legs are solid and muscular, with clean joints, clearly defined tendons, short pasterns, and tough, well-formed hooves.
History The breed descends from a French stallion called Nonius, sired by an English halfbred and out of a Norman mare. Although not particularly beautiful in appearance, this horse was to prove exceptional at stud. He was put to a wide variety of mares, Andalusian, Arab, Kladruber, Norman, and English halfbred, proving not only prolific, but also capable of leaving his unmistakable stamp on all his progeny. The Small Nonius, not very pleasing in appearance, but versatile, derives from the English Thoroughbred, while the Large Nonius, deriving from the Anglo-Norman, is still valued today as a carriage horse.

44 FURIOSO-NORTH STAR

Breed Furioso-North Star.
Place of origin Hungary.
Geographical distribution Hungary, Czechoslovakia, Poland, Romania, Austria.
Aptitudes Riding horse and light draft.
Qualities Strong and hardy.
Temperament Quiet but energetic.
Conformation A horse of the meso-dolichomorphic type, standing 16–16·2 hands (1·60–1·65 m) at the withers; the coat may be bay, brown or black. The head, well-proportioned and well set-on, has a straight profile. The neck is well-formed, quite long and with a flowing mane; the withers are prominent, the back long and straight, the croup well-muscled and slightly sloping, the tail long and well set-on, the chest wide and deep, and the shoulder well-muscled, long and sloping. The legs have good muscle structure, solid, clean joints, clearly defined, resistant tendons and tough, well-formed hooves; good natural stance.
History The breed is traced back to the nineteenth century, when the famous Hungarian stud farm of Mezöhegyes imported two stallions from England, the Norfolk Roadster North Star (1844) and the English Thoroughbred Furioso (1836). These two stallions, crossed with mares of Nonius derivation, gave rise to two distinct families, which have now lost their individuality. As a result the breed is now known by the names of its two foundation sires. This aesthetically pleasing horse was valued in the past as a carriage horse, and is equally highly regarded today as a sporting horse suited to a wide range of events.

45 EAST BULGARIAN

Breed East Bulgarian.
Place of origin Bulgaria.
Aptitudes Riding horse and light draft.
Qualities Stamina, good jumper.
Temperament Quiet but energetic.
Conformation A horse of the mesomorphic type, standing 15–16 hands (1·50–1·60 m) at the withers; the usual colors are chestnut and black. The head is light and well set-on, the profile straight, and the eyes lively. The neck is quite long and well-formed; the withers are prominent, the back long and straight, the croup slightly sloping, the tail well set-on, the chest full and deep, and the shoulder nicely sloping and well-muscled. The legs are solid and slender, with good muscular development, the tendons clean, and the foot well-shaped and tough.
History The breed is of recent formation, going back only to the end of the nineteenth century. Its development was undertaken at the Vassil Kolarov stud farm, near Shumen, by crossing English Thoroughbreds, English halfbreds, Arabs and Anglo-Arabs; once the desired characteristics had been established, only the English Thoroughbred was used to upgrade the stock. An elegant, well-built horse, the East Bulgarian is eminently well-suited to a wide variety of competitive sports, from dressage to cross-country.

46 PLEVEN

Breed Pleven.
Place of origin Bulgaria.
Geographical distribution Bulgaria.
Aptitudes Riding horse, farm work.
Qualities Good jumper.
Conformation A horse of the dolichomorphic type, standing approximately 15·2 hands (1·55 m) at the withers; the coat is chestnut. The head is well-proportioned, with a straight profile. The neck is quite long and well-muscled; the withers are high, the back long and straight, the croup slightly sloping, the chest well-developed, wide and deep, the abdomen drawn in, and the shoulder long and nicely sloping. The legs are well-structured, with broad, clean joints, long and well-muscled forearm and shin, long cannons, strong, clearly defined tendons; and well-formed feet; good natural stance.
History This breed was created at the end of the nineteenth century at the Georgi Dimitrov agricultural establishment near Pleven in Bulgaria. It is in fact an Anglo-Arab, created as a result of crosses between Russian Anglo-Arab stallions and Arab purebred, or local halfbred mares. For the following twenty-five years, until 1938, only Arab and Gidran stallions were used; once the features of the breed were considered fixed, English Thoroughbred blood was introduced. The physical build of the Pleven, together with its good jumping skills, make it an exceptional all-round sporting horse.

47 DANUBIAN

Breed Danubian.
Place of origin Bulgaria.
Geographical distribution Bulgaria.
Aptitudes Light draft and riding horse.
Qualities Strong and enduring.
Temperament Docile but energetic.
Conformation A horse of the meso-dolichomorphic type, standing approximately 15·2 hands (1·54 m) at the withers; the coat is usually black or chestnut. The head is well-proportioned, with a straight profile. The neck is of average length, strong and broad at the base; the withers are prominent, the back straight and quite long, the croup slightly sloping, the tail well set-on, the chest wide and deep, and the shoulder somewhat sloping, but powerful. The legs are long and slender, with a rather long forearm, short cannons and pasterns, and a well-formed hoof.
History The breed is of recent formation, having been initiated at the start of the twentieth century by crossing Nonius stallions with Gidran mares. The result is a fairly powerful light draft horse, also suitable as a riding horse. It is a solidly built animal, not particularly pleasing in appearance. The mares of the breed, crossed with English Thoroughbred stallions, produce good jumpers.

48 MALAPOLSKI

Breed Malapolski (Polish Anglo-Arab).
Place of origin Poland.
Geographical distribution Poland.
Aptitudes Riding horse and light draft.
Qualities Great stamina, good jumper.
Temperament Calm and well-balanced.
Conformation A horse of the dolichomorphic type, standing 15·3–16·2 hands (1·55–1·62 m) at the withers; the coat may be bay, brown, black, chestnut, gray or roan. The head is well-proportioned with a straight profile. The neck is of a good length; the withers are prominent, the back long and straight, the croup slightly sloping, the chest wide and deep, and the shoulder long and sloping. The legs are long and well-muscled, with good joints, and the foot well-formed, with tough horn.
History This relatively recent breed has been greatly influenced by Oriental blood; in addition to the English Thoroughbred, the Furioso and the Gidran have contributed to its formation. There are two distinct versions: the Sadecki, mainly influenced by the Furioso, and the Darbowsko-Tarnowski, which has received a more decisive contribution from the Gidran. This breed has points of similarity with another Polish horse, the Wielkopolski, with the difference that its appearance varies greatly according to the region in which it is reared. In general this is a noteworthy horse that performs well in sporting competitions, owing to its good jumping qualities.

---

49 WIELKOPOLSKI

Breed Wielkopolski.
Place of origin Poland.
Aptitudes Riding horse and light draft.
Qualities Sturdy build.
Temperament Well-balanced, quiet and hard-working.
Conformation A horse of the mesomorphic type, standing 15·1–16·1 hands (1·54–1·64 m) at the withers; the coat may be bay, brown, black, gray or chestnut. The head is well-formed, with a straight profile, lively eyes, and flared nostrils. The neck is well-proportioned, slightly arched, and well set-on; the withers are quite pronounced, the back straight and fairly long, the croup slightly sloping, the chest high and deep, the abdomen drawn in, and the shoulder long, well-muscled and nicely sloping. The joints of the legs are broad and clean, the forearm and shin long and well-muscled, the cannons also rather long, the tendons clean and well-defined, pasterns nicely sloping, and the foot well-formed.
History This recently developed breed descends from the Poznan, the Masuren and other formerly distinct regional types. All these horses were dual-purpose animals, with Arab, Hanoverian, East Prussian and English Thoroughbred blood. Some of these earlier breeds, although no longer officially recognized, still exist in the form of regional types living alongside the Wielkopolski. An early-maturing animal, with a free-flowing and efficient action, the Wielkopolski reflects the important contribution made to the formation of the breed by Oriental and Trakehner stallions.

50   AKHAL-TEKÉ

Breed Akhal-Teké.
Place of origin Soviet Union (Turkmenistan).
Aptitudes Riding horse.
Qualities Speed, stamina, good jumper.
Temperament Lively and courageous, sometimes stubborn and rebellious.
Conformation A horse of the meso-dolichomorphic type, standing 14·2–15·2 hands (1·44–1·54 m) at the withers; the coat may be bay, gray, black or yellow dun, often with golden highlights; there are occasional white markings. The head is light and well set-on, with a straight profile, broad forehead, long and mobile ears, lively and expressive eyes, a slender muzzle, and flared nostrils. The neck is long and well-formed (occasionally slightly swan-necked); the withers are clean and pronounced, the back long and straight, the croup slightly sloping, the chest, though not full, is in proportion, the abdomen tucked up, and the shoulder sloping. The legs are long and strong, with broad, clean joints, clearly defined tendons, long pasterns, and a well-formed foot. The skin is thin, with short, soft, silky hair; the mane is short and sparse, also extremely fine.
History The breed is thought to descend from the ancient Turkmene horse, now extinct. Reared in the Soviet Republics of Central Asia, this is an undemanding horse adapted to all climates. In 1935 horses of this breed were used for the long trek from Ashkhabad to Moscow (250 miles/400 km) across the Karakum desert. This distance was covered in just three days and completed without any water en route. The Akhal-Teké has a full-flowing and supple action, as well as an outstanding aptitude for speed, and excellent endurance.

51   DON

Breed Don.
Place of origin Soviet Union.
Aptitudes Riding horse and light draft.
Qualities Strong and hardy.
Temperament Quiet but energetic.
Conformation A horse of the meso-dolichomorphic type, standing 15·1–15·3 hands (1·55–1·65 m) at the withers; the coat may be bay, brown, black, gray or chestnut. Thje head is of average size, well set-on, with a straight profile, and large, expressive eyes. The neck is of average length and well-formed; the withers are high, the back long and straight, the croup long and slightly sloping, the chest wide and deep, and the shoulder generally sloping and well-formed. The legs are long and well-muscled, the joints broad and clean, tendons strong, and the foot broad with tough horn.
History This horse descends from the old Don horse, which was not very tall, but energetic and sturdy. It was improved in the eighteenth century by crossing with Karabair, Karabakh and Turkmene stallions. Early in the nineteenth century the breed saw the introduction of Orlov blood, followed by English Thoroughbred blood towards the end of the century. Its name derives from the river that crosses the steppes region in which this horse finds its ideal environment. The Don plays an important rôle in Soviet horse breeding, being used to improve or create other breeds, such as the Budyonny.

52 BUDYONNY

Breed Budyonny.
Place of origin Soviet Union (Rostov).
Geographical distribution Soviet Union.
Aptitudes Riding horse and light draft.
Qualities Good jumper.
Temperament Docile but energetic.
Conformation A horse of the meso-dolichomorphic type, standing 15·1–16 hands (1·55–1·62 m) at the withers; the coat is generally chestnut, but may be bay, gray, or more rarely, brown or black. The head is well-proportioned and well set-on, the profile straight or slightly snub-nosed. The neck is long and well-formed; the withers are pronounced and clean, the back long and straight, the croup slightly sloping, the tail well set-on, the chest wide and deep, and the shoulder long and sloping. The legs are long and strong, with good bone and muscle structure, solid joints, clean, well-defined tendons, and a strong well-formed hoof.
History This breed was formed by Marshal Budyonny (or Budenny), a hero of the Russian Revolution, whose intentions were to create a good horse for military use. The task was undertaken in the years following the downfall of the Tsar at the military stud farm at Rostov. The breed was formed by crossing the Don horse with the English Thoroughbred and has been officially recognized since 1948. The Budyonny has a free and natural action at all paces, especially at the gallop; this quality, coupled with its great jumping ability, makes it a versatile sporting horse well able to meet all modern requirements.

53 IOMUD

Breed Iomud (Jomud – Yomud).
Place of origin Soviet Union (Turkmenistan).
Geographical distribution Soviet Union.
Aptitudes Riding horse, light draft.
Qualities Strong, good endurance, a good jumper.
Temperament Patient but energetic.
Conformation A horse of the meso-dolichomorphic type, standing 14·1–15 hands (1·45–1·52 m) at the withers; the coat is usually gray, but sometimes chestnut, bay or black. The head is light and well-shaped, with a straight or slightly convex profile, pointed ears, and large eyes. The neck is well-formed, rather thick, and of average length; the withers are fairly prominent, the back long and straight, slightly depressed towards the withers, the croup slightly sloping, the chest deep, the abdomen tucked up, and the shoulder sloping. The legs are solid and muscular, with broad, clean joints, clearly defined tendons, and strong, well-formed hooves.
History This horse, which is a natural descendant of the ancient Turkmene, is exceptionally resistant to the arid heat of the desert, and able to survive without water for long periods. It is a solidly built horse, although it is more compact and less rangy than the Turkoman and the Akhal-Teké, which are of similar origin. In sport the Iomud is well-suited to cross-country racing, where its abilities as a jumper, combined with its extraordinary endurance, show to good advantage.

54   TURKOMAN

Breed Turkoman (Turkmen, Turkmene).
Place of origin Soviet Union (Turkmenistan).
Geographical distribution Soviet Union
Aptitudes Riding horse.
Qualities Speed and endurance.
Temperament Docile.
Conformation A horse of the dolichomorphic type, standing approximately 15 hands (1·52 m) at the withers; the coat may be gray, bay, brown black or chestnut. The head is well-proportioned and well set-on, with a straight profile, broad forehead and long ears. The neck is long and muscular; the withers are well-defined, the back long and straight, the croup long and sloping, the chest deep, and the shoulder sloping, long and muscular. The legs are long and slender, but strong and muscular, the pasterns long, and the hoof small but strong; the skin is fine.
History The Turkoman is the horse bred in Turkmenistan. It has been bred there for centuries and is the subject of many legends having been used by such great leaders as Darius and Alexander. Its modern representatives are the Akhal-Teké and the Iomud, but the Turkoman itself is extinct as a breed. Horses bred in the area are still referred to by this name and are used for flat racing, having exceptional speed as well as endurance. Proud and elegant in their bearing, these animals have a flowing and supple action.

55   MÉTIS TROTTER

Breed Métis Trotter (Russian Trotter).
Place of origin Soviet Union.
Aptitudes Trotting racing.
Qualities Good speed and reasonable stamina.
Temperament Docile and energetic.
Conformation A horse of the dolichomorphic type, standing 15·1–15·3 hands (1·55–1·60 m) at the withers; the coat may be gray, bay, brown black or chestnut. The horse is well-proportioned and well set-on, with a straight or slightly convex profile. The neck is long and muscular, well set-on; the withers are prominent, the back long and straight the croup also long and slightly sloping, the chest wide and deep, the abdomen rather tucked up, and the shoulder long, well-muscled and sloping. The legs are solid with clean joints, the forearm long, the cannons short, and the tendons clearly defined.
History This horse is the result of crossing the Orlov with the American Trotter (Standardbred), with the aim of improving its competitive performance. This programme was begun at the start of the twentieth century and the breed was officially recognized in 1949. The Métis Trotter has a flowing, far-reaching action that enables it to move quickly at a trotting pace. The limbs, especially at the back, are frequently slightly knock-kneed, causing the hind feet to move outward in a semicircular movement. This defect, known as "dishing" is, however, an advantage in that it allows the horse to find its pace more easily when lengthening its stride. While undoubtedly faster than the Orlov, this horse does not reach the standards of the faster European and American trotters.

Breed Orlov.

Place of origin Soviet Union.

Geographical distribution Soviet Union.

Aptitudes Trotting races, light draft, farm work.

Qualities Strong and enduring, great stamina.

Temperament Docile but energetic.

Conformation A horse of good conformation of the meso-dolichomorphic type, standing 15·1–17 hands (1·51–1·72 m) at the withers. The most usual coats are gray (often dappled), bay, black, and chestnut (rare). The head is well-proportioned and well set-on, with a straight profile, broad forehead, and lively eyes. The neck is long and muscular, slightly arched and well set-on; the withers are fairly pronounced, the back long, the loins strong, the croup a little elongated and slightly sloping, the tail well set-on, the chest wide and deep, and the shoulder very straight, long and muscular. The legs are sturdy, with good muscle structure, solid, clean joints, long forearm and leg; the cannons are also long and of a good thickness, the tendons clean and well-defined, and the hoof well-formed.

History In return for his help in the conspiracy to depose the future Peter III and gain the Russian throne for the Tsarina Catherine (II) the Great, Count Alexei Orlov was made commander of the Russian fleet. In his new rôle, Orlov won an important victory over the Turkish navy, on which occasion the Turkish admiral paid homage to Orlov's chivalrous conduct by giving him an Arab stallion named Smetanka. Count Orlov had this stallion crossed with several Danish and Dutch Harddraver mares, but after only one season Smetanka died. In 1778 a Danish mare with a dun coat, who had been covered by Smetanka, produced a stallion called Polkan. Polkan was in turn mated with a Danish mare, and the result was a phenomenal trotting horse called Bars 1 (1784) who is regarded as the progenitor of the breed. By a strict process of selection, involving the use of Danish, Dutch, English, Russian, Polish, and Arab mares, together with important contributions from various English Thoroughbred stallions, the distinctive characteristics of this breed, named after Count Orlov, were established. In 1865 the Stud Book was founded, and was initially open to horses of any breed that had achieved times of under two minutes over a kilometer. Now registration is restricted solely to subjects whose sire and dam are already entered in the book. The Orlov Trotter has contributed to the formation of other trotting breeds, and, in fact, at the end of the nineteenth century a number of mares were imported into France, while many horses were introduced into Italian and German studs. The Orlov has also made remarkable contributions to the development and improvement of other breeds, among them the Don. Because of its sturdiness the Orlov is used for light draft and farm work. As a racing trotter, having once swept the field in the second half of the nineteenth century, it has now given way to the French Trotter and the American trotter (Standardbred), with which it can no longer compete in terms of speed. Notwithstanding, it still competes today on Russian racecourses in races reserved for the breed. Of all the great champions of the breed, Ulov (1928) is perhaps the most outstanding, having, at the age of five, trotted a distance of 1,600 meters (1 mile) in 2'05"1.

57 NOVOKIRGHIZ

Breed Novokirghiz (New Kirghiz).
Place of origin Soviet Union.
Geographical distribution Soviet Union (Kirghizstan).
Aptitudes Riding horse, light draft, pack horse.
Qualities Strong and enduring.
Temperament Docile but energetic.
Conformation A horse of the mesomorphic type, standing 14·1–15·1 hands (1·45–1·54 m) at the withers; the coat may be bay, brown, gray or chestnut. The head is small and well-formed, with a straight profile, pointed ears, and lively eyes. The neck is long and well-formed; the withers are pronounced, the back long and straight, the croup slightly sloping, the chest well-developed, and the shoulder nicely sloping. The legs are quite short, but solid and well-muscled, with well-defined joints and tendons, and a hard and well-formed hoof.
History Descended from the old Kirghiz, which was bred in the past by nomadic tribesmen. The new breed was formed between 1930 and 1940, thanks to infusions of blood firstly from the English Thoroughbred, and then from the Don. Later, halfbred Anglo-Don blood was introduced. Through these stages the characteristics of the breed were finally determined. Originally from the mountains of Soviet Central Asia, and China, this horse is able to cope with all kinds of terrain, however rough and uneven.

---

58 UKRAINIAN RIDING HORSE

Breed Ukrainian Riding Horse.
Place of origin Soviet Union (Ukraine).
Aptitudes Riding horse, light draft, farm work.
Qualities Good competition horse.
Temperament Genial.
Conformation A horse of the meso-dolichomorphic type, the height at the withers being approximately 16·1 hands (1·64 m) in the males and 15·1 hands (1·55 m) in the females. The coat is usually chestnut, bay or black. The head is rather large, with a straight profile, well-proportioned and pricked-up ears, lively eyes, and flared nostrils. The neck is long and well-muscled; the withers are high, the back slightly hollow towards the withers, the croup long and slightly sloping, the chest deep, and the shoulder long and sloping. The legs are sturdy, with broad joints, long forearm and well-proportioned foot.
History The breed was created in the years immediately following World War II, by crossing Trakehner, Hanoverian and English Thoroughbred stallions with local mares, or with Nonius, Furioso-North Star and Gidran mares from Hungary. Later, selection continued using only English Thoroughbred and Hanoverian stallions, or English halfbreds produced from crossing Hanoverians and English Thoroughbreds. The colts are broken in at eighteen months and selected by means of aptitude tests (flat racing, cross-country, show jumping or dressage), and the best sent as breeding stock to state-owned stud farms. A good competition horse, well-suited also to light draft, and farm work.

59 TERSKY

Breed Tersky (Tersk – Terskij – Terek).
Place of origin Soviet Union (Stavropol).
Aptitudes Riding horse and light draft.
Qualities Good jumper.
Temperament Docile and intelligent.
Conformation A horse of the meso-dolichomorphic type, standing 14·3–15·1 hands (1·50–1·54 m) at the withers; the females may be smaller, sometimes measuring under 14·1 hands (1·45 m). The coat is always gray. The head is well-proportioned, with a straight or slightly snub profile, the ears are average size, pointed and mobile, and the eyes large and lively. The neck is of average length and well-formed; the withers are pronounced, the back straight and not too long, the croup rather flat, the tail set-on high, the chest wide and deep, and the shoulder long and sloping. The legs are well-built and well-muscled, joints and tendons well-defined, the foot well-conformed.
History This breed can be traced back to the old Tersky used by the Cossacks, which was significantly improved in the nineteenth century by Count Strovanov, using infusions of Kabardin blood. It was later perfected by Marshal Budyonny who introduced blood again from the Kabardin, as well as from the Don, the Arab, and the English Thoroughbred. The breed was officially recognized in 1948. Originally created for military use, it has become increasingly important in sporting events. Because of its natural aptitude for jumping, the Tersky has given excellent results in show jumping, cross-country and dressage. It is bred at the state studs of Stavropol and Tersk.

---

60 KARABAIR

Breed Karabair.
Place of origin Soviet Union (Uzbekistan).
Aptitudes Riding horse, light draft.
Qualities Vigorous, agile and enduring.
Temperament Sensitive and patient.
Conformation A horse of the mesomorphic type, standing 14·2–15 hands (1·47–1·52 m) at the withers; in the female the lower limit may be reduced to 14·1 hands (1·44 m). The coat may be gray, chestnut or bay, more rarely brown and black. The head is small but with rather pronounced jaws, a straight profile, long ears, set well apart, large, lively eyes, and flared nostrils. The neck is well-muscled and a good length; the withers are prominent, the back straight and not too long, the croup muscular and sloping, the chest wide and deep, and the shoulder sloping and well-muscled. The legs are solid, with good bone structure, the joints broad, the tendons strong, and the foot small, with tough horn.
History This horse is of very ancient origin, and its appearance suggests that it must be descended from the Arab. It is bred in three distinct types, almost identical in size: a heavy version, for light draft work or for use as a riding or pack horse, a lighter riding horse and a third with longer lines better adapted to draft work. Very resistant to cold and fatigue, it is well-suited to mountainous regions, its sure-footedness enabling it to negotiate the steepest and most demanding tracks. Its wide range of useful qualities has led to its use in the improvement of other breeds, and it has contributed to the development of the Don.

61 KABARDIN

Breed Kabardin.
Place of origin Soviet Union (Caucasus).
Aptitudes Riding and pack horse.
Qualities Long-lived, frugal, agile, strong and enduring.
Temperament Calm and responsive, but energetic.
Conformation A horse of the mesomorphic type, standing 14·1–15·1 hands (1·45–1·54 m) at the withers; the coat may be bay, brown, black or gray. The head is nicely proportioned but with rather pronounced jaws, a straight or slightly convex profile, and long ears, with the points turned inward. The neck is quite long and muscular, with a flowing mane; the withers are not very high, but long, the back is short and straight, the loins short, the croup sloping, the tail full and set-on quite low, the chest wide and deep, and the shoulder rather straight but well-muscled. The legs are solid, with clean joints, clearly defined tendons, and a well-formed foot.
History The origins of this breed almost certainly trace back to the Arab and the Turkmene, as can be seen from its typically Oriental features. It is a perfect horse for steep, mountainous country, gifted with a well-developed sense of direction. The Kabardin has strength and endurance, and is sure-footed and agile. These qualities are inborn, the place of origin of the breed being in the Caucasian mountains. Outside its natural habitat it shows great ability as a sporting horse. In the past it has been used in the improvement of other breeds, such as the Tersky.

---

62 KARABAKH

Breed Karabakh.
Place of origin Soviet Union (Azerbaijan).
Aptitudes Riding and pack horse.
Qualities Strong and enduring.
Temperament Calm but energetic.
Conformation A horse of the mesomorphic type, standing 14–14·1 hands (1·43–1·45 m) at the withers; the coat is generally golden dun (with eel stripe), chestnut, bay or gray, with possible white markings, and mane and tail of a darker color. The head is small and well set-on, with a straight profile, expressive eyes, flared nostrils, and a soft muzzle. The neck is long and well-formed; the withers are prominent, the back long and straight, the flanks well-formed, the croup sloping, the tail set-on slightly low, the chest deep, and the shoulder sloping but a little flat. The legs are solid, with good bone and muscle, clean joints, clearly defined tendons, and a well-formed foot with tough horn.
History This breed goes back a long way and shows a strong Oriental influence; it seems to have received important infusions of Arab, Persian and Turkmene blood. It originated in the mountains separating Azerbaijan from northwest Iran. A sure-footed animal, it has no fear of harsh terrain, and proves a perfect horse for rugged, mountainous country. Because of its distinctive bearing as well as its physical qualities, it has been used to improve other breeds, among them the Don.

63 LOKAI

Breed Lokai.
Place of origin Soviet Union (Tadzhikistan).
Geographical distribution Soviet Union.
Aptitudes Riding and pack horse.
Qualities Agile, with good endurance.
Temperament Docile and willing.
Conformation A horse of the mesomorphic type, standing 14–14·2 hands (1·42–1·47 m) at the withers; the coat is generally chestnut (with brilliant golden highlights), bay or gray, with black and dun occurring more rarely. The head is well-proportioned and well set-on, with a straight or slightly convex profile, small ears, and lively eyes. The neck is quite long and well-formed; the withers are fairly prominent, the back short and straight, the croup sloping, the tail set-on quite low, the chest is wide and deep, and the shoulder sloping and muscular. The legs are solid, with good bone and muscle, clean joints, and clearly defined tendons; the pasterns are a good length and nicely sloping, and the foot well-formed with tough horn.
History This breed dates back to the sixteenth century and has a varied ancestry that includes contributions from the Iomud, the Karabair, and the Arab, all of which breeds had a considerable influence on local horse populations; its noble origins are revealed in its good conformation and proud bearing. The horse comes from the mountainous regions of Tadzhikistan, in which it is well able to demonstrate its qualities. Away from its native environment it proves an excellent riding horse well-suited to competitive sports.

---

64 TORIC

Breed Toric.
Place of origin Soviet Union (Estonia).
Aptitudes Farm work, light and medium draft.
Qualities Willing, good endurance.
Temperament Calm and patient.
Conformation A horse of the mesomorphic type, standing 15–15·1 hands (1·52–1·55 m) at the withers; the coat is generally chestnut, bay, brown or gray, with possible white markings. The head is of average size and well set-on, with a straight profile and long ears. The neck is quite long and muscular; the withers are low, the back short, wide and muscular, sometimes slightly hollow, the loins strong, the croup slightly sloping, the tail well set-on, the chest wide and deep, with well-rounded ribs, and the shoulder sloping but very large and muscular. The legs are short and solid, with broad, clean joints, short cannons and pasterns, strong tendons, and an an average-sized foot, with tough horn.
History Of fairly recent origin, this breed was developed in the nineteenth century by crossing a variety of breeds, including the Arab, the Ardennais, the Hackney, the East Frisian, the Hanoverian, the Orlov, the English Thoroughbred and the Trakehner, with the Klepper, an old indigenous draft breed descended from the Arab and the Ardennais. It is for this reason that this horse is also known as the Estonian Klepper and the Double Klepper. An attractive-looking horse, betraying its noble origins, the Toric is well-suited to draft and farm work.

65 LATVIAN

Breed Latvian (Latvian Harness Horse).
Place of origin Soviet Union (Latvia).
Aptitudes Riding horse, farm work, light and heavy draft.
Qualities Strong, good endurance.
Temperament Docile and calm.
Conformation A horse of the mesomorphic type, standing 15·1–16 hands (1·54–1·62 m) at the withers; the coat may be black, gray, chestnut, bay or brown. The head is rather large, with a straight profile, full forelock, small ears, and gentle eyes. The neck is long and muscular, with a flowing mane; the withers are fairly prominent, the back straight, the croup long and slightly sloping, the tail long and full, the chest high and deep, and the shoulder long and sloping. The legs are rather short, but solid and well-muscled, with broad, strong joints, some feather on the rear of the cannons and fetlocks, and a well-formed foot.
History This breed probably dates back to prehistoric times and its resemblance to the North Swedish Horse and to the Døle Gudbrandsdal would suggest that all these breeds derive from the same ancient stock that has given rise to all the heavy draft breeds of northern Europe. Since the seventeenth century the breed has received infusions of blood from German riding horses, the Arab and, more recently, the English Thoroughbred. The breed can be considered to have been firmly established since 1952. In addition to the standard type, known as the Latvian Harness Horse, there is a lighter version, sometimes known as the Latvian Riding Horse, and a heavier version, better suited to draft work.

---

66 KUSTANAIR

Breed Kustanair.
Place of origin Soviet Union (Kazakhstan).
Geographical distribution Soviet Union (Kazakhstan).
Aptitudes Riding horse and light draft.
Qualities Versatile, strong, good endurance, frugal.
Temperament Calm but energetic.
Conformation A horse of the mesomorphic type, standing 15–15·1 hands (1·52–1·54 m) at the withers; the coat may be bay, brown, black, chestnut, gray or roan. The head is quite light, the profile straight, the forehead broad, the eyes small, and the lower jaw well-defined. The neck is of average length and muscular; the withers are also muscular and quite prominent, the back is long and straight, the croup sloping, the chest wide and deep, and the shoulder long and sloping. The legs are long and well-muscled, with good bone structure, clean joints, and a well-formed foot.
History An ancient Oriental breed, now produced in two distinct types: one, which is light and elegant in appearance, having been improved by crosses with the English Thoroughbred; the other a more solid version obtained by crossing with the Orlov and the Don horse.

67 KARACABEY

Breed Karacabey.
Place of origin Turkey.
Geographical distribution Turkey.
Aptitudes Riding and pack horse, medium-light draft, farm work.
Qualities Good endurance, versatile.
Temperament Steady and willing.
Conformation A horse of the mesomorphic type, standing 15·1–16·1 hands (1·55–1·64 m) at the withers; the coat may be bay, brown, black, gray, roan or chestnut. The head is well-proportioned, the profile straight, the ears upright, and the eyes lively. The neck is well-proportioned and slightly arched; the withers are quite pronounced, the back straight, the croup rounded and muscular, the tail well set-on, the chest wide and deep, and the shoulder sloping. The legs are solid and strong, with good bone structure and joints, well-defined tendons, and a well-formed foot, with tough horn.
History This horse originated from crosses made at the beginning of the twentieth century between local mares and Nonius stallions. The result was a versatile horse, with good conformation used in the past by the Turkish cavalry. It is the only Turkish breed to display uniformity of type and constant transmission of characteristics.

68 MORGAN

Breed Morgan.
Place of origin United States.
Aptitudes Light draft and riding horse.
Qualities Versatile, fast, good endurance.
Temperament Docile but energetic.
Conformation An elegant horse of the mesomorphic type, standing 14–15·1 hands (1·42–1·54 m) at the withers, and weighing 800–1,100 lb (400–500 kg). The coat is usually bay, chestnut or black, with frequent white markings. The head is of average size, with a straight profile, small, pointed ears, well-spaced, expressive eyes, and flared nostrils. The neck is of average length, muscular and arched; the withers are well defined but not very high, the back wide and short, the loins strong, the croup quite long and rounded, the tail well set-on, the chest wide and deep, and the shoulder long, sloping and muscular. The legs are solid, with good bone structure, the cannons short, the tendons well-defined, the pasterns not too sloping, and the foot well-proportioned.
History The foundation sire of the breed was Justin Morgan, a small bay of barely 14 hands (1.42 m), foaled in 1790 in Massachusetts. Sired by an English Thoroughbred and out of a mare of mixed Arab, Welsh Cob, Harddraver and Fjord blood, he was named after his second owner Thomas Justin Morgan. On Morgan's death, he went to a farmer who entered him in weight-pulling competitions where he earned a reputation for being invincible. His most outstanding achievement, however was as a sire at stud. Once used in trotting races itself, the Morgan has contributed to the creation of the American trotter (Standardbred).

Breed Quarter Horse.

Place of origin United States.

Geographical distribution United States and some European countries.

Aptitudes Riding horse, sprint races.

Qualities Agile, fast, quick off the mark.

Temperament Docile, but lively and energetic, exceptionally well-balanced.

Conformation A sturdy, powerfully-built horse, medium-sized, and of the dolichomorphic type, standing 14·1–16 hands (1·54–1·63 m) at the withers, and weighing 940–1,210 lb (425–550 kg). The colors of the coat are very varied, many of them, and their names, being peculiar to the breed. They may be sorrel, chestnut, bay, brown, black, liver chestnut, dun, red dun, buckskin, grullo (a type of mouse dun), palomino, gray, blue roan or red roan. The Quarter Horse has a short, broad head, with a straight profile, a wide forehead, ears of average length, pricked, and set well apart; the eyes are large and reflect the calm yet lively nature of the animal. The neck is muscular, well-formed, and slightly arched; the withers are well-defined and quite prominent, the back short and straight, the croup long, muscular and rounded, dropping gently to the haunches and to the tail, which is set-on quite low; the chest is wide and deep, and the shoulder long, sloping and muscular. The legs are solid and well-formed, with broad, clean joints, very muscular thighs, short cannons, clean and well-defined tendons, pasterns of medium length and rather straight, and a well-formed foot, with tough horn.

History This horse was developed in the seventeenth century, when the first settlers in Virginia and Carolina embarked on a selection process, crossing mares of Andalusian descent with English horses that they had brought over with them. These horses already had the characteristics of the English Thoroughbred, but could not be described as such, since the breed had not yet been officially recognized. Subsequent selection was based on the performance of the horses in sprint races held along the main street of the village over a distance of a quarter of a mile; hence the name of the breed. The aim of these settlers had been to produce a fast, lively horse, agile and with very quick reflexes, which could be used by herdsmen for rounding up cattle. The results were surprisingly good and the new breed seemed to have a natural ability for the work. It is these same qualities that make the Quarter Horse still an ideal mount for rodeos today. Apart from its aptitude for sprint races over very short distances (300–880 yd/274–800 m) in which no other horse in the world can beat it, the Quarter Horse is also used for cattle work, polo, show jumping and hunting, its versatile nature making it a top class sporting animal. The Stud Book is kept by the American Quarter Horse Association, which has its headquarters at Amarillo in Texas.

Breed Standardbred (American Trotter).
Place of origin United States.
Geographical distribution United States, Canada, Europe, New Zealand, Australia.
Aptitudes Trotting races, pacing races.
Qualities Great speed.
Temperament Willing and competitive.
Conformation A horse of the dolichomorphic type, standing 14·1–16·1 hands (1·45–1·65 m) at the withers, and weighing 790–1,170 lb (360–580 kg). The coat may be bay (most frequent), brown, black or chestnut; gray and roan occur more rarely. The head is of medium size, with a straight or slightly convex profile, rather pronounced jaws, long ears, and lively and expressive eyes. The neck is long and muscular and well set-on; the withers are prominent and muscular, the back straight and long, the loins short, the croup long, broad and sloping, the chest wide and deep, the abdomen quite tucked up, and the shoulder well-muscled, long and sloping. The legs are strong, the joints broad and clean, the thigh muscular, the forearm long, the cannons not too long, but with strong, clearly defined tendons, the pasterns long, and the foot well-formed and with tough horn. The skin is fine.
History The Standardbred breed comprises both pacers and trotters. Pacing is a faster gait than trotting and is consequently not permitted in trotting races. In the United States there are separate events for pacers, and as their popularity has increased, so has the demand for the Standardbred. The foundation sire of the breed was the English Thoroughbred stallion Messenger (gr. 1780), imported into the United States when he was eight years old. Directly, or through his descendants, this stallion has a determining influence on an important nucleus of trotting and pacing mares, which had already been carefully selected, although from a variety of different breeds. Messenger was directly descended in the male line from Sampson, who played a decisive rôle in the formation of trotting breeds, particularly in France, by the transmission of his particular aptitude for trotting to all his progeny. In the direct male line from Messenger and in the third generation is the famous stallion Hambletonian 10, from whom all present-day Standardbreds descend. Other strains that contributed to the creation of the breed, such as the Mambrinos (also descended from Messenger), the Clays, and the Morgans (descended from Justin Morgan) did not succeed in perpetuating a direct male line down to the present day. Another stallion who contributed to the formation of the breed was Norfolk Bellfounder (b.1817), imported into the States when he was a five-year-old. Of the 1,300 foals sired by Hambletonian 10, the onus of perpetuating the breed fell on only three, giving rise to the four current blood strains: Happy Medium (br.1863), from whom descends the line headed by Peter the Great; Electioneer (br.1868), from whom the Bingen line descends; George Wilkes (br.1856), from whom the Axworthy and McKinney lines descend. The Standardbred is prized for its ability to put on short bursts of speed, the logical outcome of a selection process based on trials over distances generally of one mile. The world record for trotting is held by Prakas (b.h.1982) who, at the age of three, trotted the mile in a time of 1′53·9″ (equivalent km time 1′10·8″). The world record for pacing is held by Niatross (b.h.1977) with a time over one mile of 1′49·2″ (1′7·8″/km), established in 1980, in a trial.

71 PINTO

Breed Pinto.
Place of origin United States.
Aptitudes Riding horse and light draft.
Qualities Robust.
Temperament Docile and quiet.
Conformation A horse of the mesomorphic type, standing 14·1–15·1 hands (1·45–1·55 m) at the withers. There are two basic types of coat, known as Overo, with white patches on a colored ground, and Tobiano, with colored patches on a white ground. This is a solidly built, compact animal, but the characteristics of the breed, apart from the coat, are poorly defined. The head should be well-proportioned, with a straight profile, a wide face, and pricked-up, average-sized ears; the neck should be well-formed and muscular, the withers moderately pronounced, the back short, the croup rounded, the tail well set-on, the chest wide and deep, the shoulder long and nicely sloping. The legs should be solid and well-muscled, quite short, with strong joints and tendons, and rounded, well-proportioned feet.
History This breed derives from horses, some of which were part-colored, which the American Indians captured from the Spanish *conquistadores*. In 1963 the American Paint Horse Association started the Stud Book. To be registered, a horse must have at least one parent already listed, and the other parent must be either a Quarter Horse or an English Thoroughbred. The foundation sires of the breed are the two stallions Sheik and Sun Cloud. The dominant coat appears to be the Tobiano.

72 APPALOOSA

Breed Appaloosa.
Place of origin United States.
Aptitudes Riding horse.
Qualities Agile, with good endurance.
Temperament Docile and quiet, but lively.
Conformation A horse of the mesomorphic type, standing 14·1–15·1 hands (1·45–1·55 m) at the withers, and weighing 880–1,280 lb (400–580 kg). There are six characteristic spotted coats, known as snowflake, leopard, frost, marble, spotted blanket, and white blanket. The head is small and well set-on, the profile straight, the ears pointed, and the eyes large, with obvious sclera. The neck is long and well-muscled, and the mane short and sparse; the withers are moderately pronounced, the back short and straight, the croup muscular and rounded, the tail short, with sparse hairs of varying length, the chest deep, and the shoulder long and sloping. The legs are solid and well-muscled, with good bone structure, and hooves characterized by vertical black and white stripes; the skin of the nose, lips and genitals is covered with gray-pink mottling.
History The Appaloosa is descended from horses introduced into America by the Spanish *conquistadores* in the sixteenth century. The name comes from the Palouse river which crossed territory occupied long ago by the Nez-Percés Indians who were the first to fix this horse's characteristics by appropriate crossing. This selection was continued by white settlers in America and, in 1938, the breed was officially recognized. The foals are born with coats of uniform color; the markings appear later and are invariably a different color from those of the parents.

73 PALOMINO

Breed Palomino.
Place of origin United States.
Aptitudes Riding horse.
Qualities Easily managed and often a good jumper.
Temperament Docile and quiet.
Conformation A horse of the mesomorphic type, standing 14–16 hands (1·43–1·62 m) at the withers, and weighing 1,100–1,145 lb (500–520 kg). The characteristic palomino coat is typically described as the color of a "newly-minted gold coin"; white markings are permitted only on the face (not exceeding the star, stripe or extended stripe) and on the lower part of the legs (below the knee and the hock); the forelock, mane and tail must be lighter or darker in color than the coat (ivory, silver, flaxen) with not more than fifteen per cent of black hairs. The head is small and well set-on, with a straight profile, small ears, and dark or hazel eyes, both of the same color. The neck is quite long and well-formed, with a resplendent mane; the withers are moderately pronounced, the back straight, the croup rounded, the tail full and well set-on, the chest deep and quite wide, and the shoulder long and sloping. The legs are well-muscled, with good bone structure, clearly defined tendons, and a well-formed foot; the skin is fine and dark.
History This horse cannot yet be regarded as an established breed, since it does not present uniform characteristics. The only feature all palominos have in common is their coat but strangely enough it is not possible to transmit this color reliably. The horse is highly regarded in the United States, and in Great Britain there is a pony version.

---

74 ALBINO

Breed Albino (American Cream).
Place of origin United States.
Aptitudes Riding horse.
Qualities Natural aptitude for learning exercises.
Temperament Docile.
Conformation A horse of the mesomorphic type, standing approximately 15·1 hands (1·54 m) at the withers, and weighing 1,100–1,145 lb (500–520 kg). The coat may be of four different color combinations: ivory-white, with a white mane (lighter than the body color), blue eyes and pink skin; cream body, the mane darker than the body, cinnamon-colored skin and dark eyes; the body and mane of the same pale cream color with blue eyes and pink skin; the body and mane of the same cream color, again with blue eyes and pink skin. Physically this horse varies greatly, and may resemble the Quarter Horse, the Morgan, the English Thoroughbred or the Arab.
History The American Albino, which originated in Nebraska in 1937, is said to descend from the stallion Old King, sired by an Arab stallion and out of a Morgan mare. The Albino does not present uniform physical characteristics and therefore is considered by many to be a color type rather than a breed. It is used as a leisure horse, as well as for film and circus work. Since 1970 a distinction has been made between the Albino (white) and the Cream, since the white coat of some Albinos did not result from the absence of pigmentation. The American Albino Horse Club changed its name in 1970 to the American White Horse Club, and the breed is now called the American Cream.

75 AMERICAN SADDLEBRED

Breed American Saddlebred (Kentucky Saddlebred, American Saddlehorse).
Place of origin United States (Kentucky).
Aptitudes Riding horse and light draft.
Qualities Strong, with good endurance.
Temperament Docile, but energetic.
Conformation A horse of the meso-dolichomorphic type, standing 15–16 hands (1·52–1·62 m) at the withers; the coat is usually bay, black, chestnut or gray, roan occurring rarely. The head is small, with a straight or slightly convex profile, pointed ears, large eyes, and flared nostrils. The neck is long, arched and muscular; the withers are prominent, the back straight and fairly long, the croup flat, the tail well set-on and carried erect due to nicking of the muscles or the nerve (myotomy or neurotomy), the chest wide and deep, and the shoulder long, sloping and well-muscled. The legs are long and slender, with good bone structure and joints, well-defined tendons, long, sloping pasterns, and a small, solid hoof, open at the heel; the natural stance is not correct, being thrust forward in front and straight-hocked at the back.
History Also known as the Kentucky Saddlebred, this horse was created as a dual-purpose riding and light draft breed, using the English Thoroughbred, the Morgan, the Narragansett Pacer and, perhaps, the Hackney. Depending on the training given, the horse can have three or five different gaits: the "three-gaited" saddlebred performs the walk, trot and canter; the "five-gaited" saddlebred can perform two additional artificial gaits: the "slow gait" or four-beat "stepping pace," and the "rack," which is similar, but faster.

76 MISSOURI FOX TROTTING HORSE

Breed Missouri Fox Trotting Horse.
Place of origin United States (Missouri and Arkansas).
Aptitudes Riding horse.
Qualities Characteristic gait.
Temperament Quiet but energetic.
Conformation A horse of the mesomorphic type, standing 14–16 hands (1·42–1·62 m) at the withers; the coat may be chestnut, bay, black, gray, piebald or skewbald. The head is well-proportioned, with a straight profile, pointed ears, and large, lively eyes. The neck is nicely proportioned and well-formed; the withers are pronounced, the back short and straight, the flanks full, the croup muscular and rounded, the tail well set-on, the chest broad, muscular and deep, and the shoulder nicely sloping and muscular. The legs are sturdy, the hoof well-formed and in proportion to the size of the horse; good natural stance.
History Although this horse has been bred in Missouri since the beginning of the nineteenth century, it still does not have clearly defined, constant characteristics. Its most salient feature is the distinctive four-beat gait, known as the "foxtrot," in which the horse canters with its forelegs and walks or trots with its hind legs. The movement of the limbs is accompanied by a rhythmic movement of the head, often producing a clearly audible beat, created by the noise of the hooves together with the chattering together of the teeth. Its steady and enduring action, enabling it to travel long distances at an average speed of 5–10 mph (8–16 kmh), makes it an ideal mount for cowboys.

77   TENNESSEE WALKING HORSE

Breed Tennessee Walking Horse.
Place of origin United States.
Aptitudes Riding horse.
Qualities Comfortable gait, good performance.
Temperament Sociable, docile and quiet, but energetic.
Conformation A horse of the mesomorphic type, standing 15–16 hands (1·52–1·62 m) at the withers; the coat may be black, bay, brown, chestnut, gray or roan. The head is rather large, with a straight profile, pointed ears, gentle eyes, and flared nostrils. The neck is arched and muscular, broad at the base; the withers are quite pronounced, but not well-defined, the back straight, quite short and strong, the loins powerful, the croup muscular and rather flat, the tail set-on high and held erect, due to nicking (myotomy or neurotomy), the chest wide, deep and muscular, and the shoulder well-muscled, long and sloping. The legs are sturdy and muscular, with good bone structure, broad joints, clearly defined tendons, and a well-proportioned and tough hoof.
History Officially recognized in 1935, this breed descends from the stallion Black Allan (1886) of Morgan and Hambletonian blood. His son, Roan Allan, with contributions from the English Thoroughbred, the Standardbred, the American Saddlebred and Canadian pacers, gave rise to the present-day Tennessee Walking Horse, which is characterized by its peculiar, four-beat "running walk." The movements of this gait, which is both fast and comfortable, are so long that the imprints of the hind feet extend beyond those of the forefeet.

78   MUSTANG

Breed Mustang (Spanish Mustang).
Place of origin United States.
Aptitudes Riding horse.
Qualities Strong, with good endurance.
Temperament Courageous, but independent and intractable.
Conformation A horse of the mesomorphic type, standing 14–15 hands (1·42–1·52 m) at the withers; the coat may be of any color or variety, but is often palomino, dun, or mouse-colored. The Mustang, as a breed, possesses little uniformity, the result of regression related to environmental factors and living conditions. The head is generally rather heavy, the neck robust, the withers low, the back short, the croup rounded, the chest wide, the shoulder straight, and the legs sturdy.
History The Mustang is derived from the horses brought over to the New World from Europe by the Spanish *conquistadores*. Some of these animals managed to escape; coming together in herds, they reproduced according to natural selection, a process whereby only the fittest survive. It is a typical example of a horse that has reverted to the wild, and this can be seen from the reappearance of the ancestral coat in some animals, and the extraordinary resistance they have acquired. This horse lives along the coasts of California and Mexico, but has been hunted so mercilessly that of the two million animals in existence at the beginning of the twentieth century, there now remain only a few thousand, enclosed in ranches; since 1957 they have been controlled and registered. The Mustang's rebellious nature is shown to great effect in the rodeo.

79 WILD HORSE OF WYOMING

Breed Wild Horse of Wyoming.
Place of origin United States (Wyoming Desert).
Geographical distribution United States (Wyoming Desert).
Aptitudes Life in the wild.
Qualities Hardiness.
Temperament Independent.
Conformation A horse of the mesomorphic type, standing 15–16 hands (1·52–1·62 m) at the withers; the coat may be of almost any color, but palomino predominates. It is very similar in build to the Mustang: the head is fairly heavy, the neck powerful, the withers low, the back short, the croup rounded, the chest wide, the shoulder straight, and the legs sturdy.
History This breed, which has settled in the Wyoming Desert, rather than being "wild," has, in fact, reverted to the wild in as far as its origins are similar to those of the Mustang. It has been influenced by Arab, Berber, Spanish, and Turkmene blood; these horses were first brought from Europe to America by Cortés and, later, by the colonists. The wild horse of Wyoming has been systematically captured and used in the formation of other American breeds, such as the Palomino and the Pinto.

80 CANADIAN CUTTING HORSE

Breed Canadian Cutting Horse.
Place of origin Canada.
Aptitudes Riding horse.
Qualities Agile, fast and quick off the mark.
Temperament Active, well-balanced.
Conformation A horse of the dolichomorphic type, standing 15·1–16·1 hands (1·54–1·64 m) at the withers; the coat may be bay, brown, black, gray and chestnut. The head is well-proportioned, with a straight or slightly convex profile. The neck is also well-proportioned and well set-on; the withers are moderately pronounced, the back straight, the croup wide and sloping, the chest broad and well-developed, and the shoulder wide and sloping. The joints of the legs are clean, the tendons strong, and the foot well-shaped with good horn; good natural stance.
History This horse derives from the Quarter Horse, which it resembles both in physical appearance asnd temperament. Invaluable to the cowboys for its skill and natural instinct for herding cattle, the Cutting Horse is also used in the various competitions that go to make up the rodeo, a sporting event that is becoming increasingly popular in Canada.

81 AZTECA

Breed Azteca.
Place of origin Mexico.
Aptitudes Riding horse, light draft, farm work.
Qualities Hardy, fast, agile.
Temperament Noble, docile, lively, well-balanced.
Conformation A horse of the mesomorphic type, with good conformation. The females must stand at least 14·3 hands (1·50 m) at the withers and the males a minimum of 15 hands (1·52 m). All coat colors are permitted, with the exclusion of part colors (piebald, skewbald and spotted). The head is lean, with a straight or slightly convex profile, small, well-pricked-up ears, and expressive eyes, not too close together. The neck is well-muscled and slightly arched, with a flowing mane; the withers are high, the back straight, the croup broad and rounded, the tail well set-on and flowing, the girth full and deep (minimum circumference 6 ft/1·80 m), and the shoulder long and sloping. The legs are well-muscled, with good joints, long, thin cannons, clearly defined tendons, and a well-proportioned foot.
History This recent breed has taken the place of the now extinct Native Mexican (Mexican criollo). Selection began in 1972 by crossing Andalusian stallions with Quarter Horse mares or vice versa, or by crossing Andalusian stallions with improved Criollo mares. It must have a minimum of ⅜ and a maximum of ⅝ of Spanish or Quarter Horse blood, while blood from horses not registered as Criollo may not exceed ¼. The purpose of producing this breed has been to combine the qualities of the Andalusian with those of the Quarter Horse. The result is an elegant horse, well-suited to competitive sports and leisure riding.

82 PASO FINO

Breed Paso Fino.
Place of origin Peru.
Aptitudes Riding horse.
Qualities Strong and willing.
Temperament Calm, but lively.
Conformation A horse of the mesomorphic type, standing 14–15·1 hands (1·42–1·54 m) at the withers; the coat may be of any color. The head is correctly proportioned, the profile straight or snub, the ears small and pointed, the eyes lively, and the nostrils flared. The neck is strong, muscular and well-formed; the withers are fairly pronounced, the back short and straight, the loins strong, the croup rounded, the tail well set-on, the chest wide and deep, and the shoulder correctly sloping. The legs are strong and sound, with short cannons and tough hooves.
History The Paso Fino is a descendant of the horses taken from Europe to America in the sixteenth century by the Spanish *conquistadores*. Its gradual adaptation to the differing environmental conditions and breeding habits, as well as crossbreeding, resulted in physical changes that eventually became part of its genetic make up. This horse is characterized by three natural, lateral, four-beat gaits: the *paso fino*, which is the slowest, the *paso corto*, the smoothest, and therefore suitable for long distances, and the *paso largo*, the fastest. Bred in Puerto Rico, Colombia and Peru, certain differences do exist between the horses from these three countries, but they are becoming less marked in the American Paso Fino bred in the United States.

Breed Criollo.
Place of origin Argentina.
Geographical distribution South America.
Aptitudes Riding horse.
Qualities Resistant, fast, good stamina.
Temperament Tenacious and willing.
Conformation A horse of the mesomorphic type, standing 14–15 hands (1·42–1·52 m) at the withers; the coat may be of any color: gray, chestnut, bay, black, roan, mouse-colored, dun and even piebald and skewbald; white markings are frequent, and some coats may have an eel stripe down the center of the back. The head is quite long, with a straight profile, broad forehead, long ears, and lively eyes. The neck is long and muscular, with a full mane; the withers are prominent, the back short and straight, the loins strong, the croup rounded, the tail full and flowing, the chest broad, and the shoulder sloping and well-muscled. The legs are solidly built, with good bone and muscle structure, the joints and tendons are strong, the pasterns long, and the hoof well-formed and robust.
History The origins of this breed go back to the early sixteenth century, when Christopher Columbus and the *conquistadores* brought Barb and Andalusian horses to South America. Having been stolen by local Indian tribes, many of these horses regained their freedom, and as a result of breeding in the wild developed excellent resistance to disease and adverse environmental conditions, and became more frugal. The Criollo, which descends from these horses, is now bred in Argentina where it is used by the *gauchos*. It is a hardy animal, with great endurance, capable of undertaking arduous treks for days without reserves of water or food. Toward the end of the nineteenth century, with the introduction of stallions imported from Europe and the United States, the breed began to deteriorate, losing its frugality and resistance to disease. However, since the beginning of the twentieth century the breed has once again been subjected to rigid selection and in 1918 the Stud Book was established. Other South American countries breed their own versions of the criollo, all of which have the same origins as the Argentinian Criollo, but different characteristics and names. The criollo reared in Chile is called the Chileno, and is similar to the Argentine Criollo, from which it descends, but is sturdier and more resistant; in Colombia it takes the name of Guajira, from the region of the same name; in Venezuela its name is Llanero and it is lighter and less solidly built, with a rather convex profile; in Peru it is described as Salteno and there are three distinct types, the Costeño, with its characteristic "paso llano" (a distinctive high-stepping gait), the Morochuco, reared in the Andes, with an occasionally protruding forehead and smaller ears, and the Chola, with a sturdier build. In Brazil there are three different breeds: the criollo of Rio Grande do Sul, of Barb-like appearance, the Mangalarga obtained by crossing the Andalusian and the Altér-Real, and the Campolino (from the name of its originator), which is of Andalusian descent and has shorter cannons and pasterns and a deeper chest than those mentioned earlier.

84 WALER

Breed Waler (Australian Stock Horse).
Place of origin Australia.
Aptitudes Riding horse and light draft.
Qualities Good jumper.
Temperament Docile and spirited.
Conformation A horse of the meso-dolichomorphic type, standing 14·2–16 hands (1·47–1·63 m) at the withers; the coat may be bay, brown, black, gray or roan. The head is well-proportioned, with a straight profile, long ears, and flared nostrils. The neck is long and well-formed; the withers are prominent, the back long and straight, the croup slightly sloping, the chest wide and deep, and the shoulder rather straight, but well-muscled. The legs are solidly built and well-muscled, with strong joints, clean tendons, and well-shaped feet.
History This breed was originally created in New South Wales by crossing Arab, English Thoroughbred and Anglo-Arab stallions with mares of various origins, including some belonging to the Cape breed, (the first breed to be introduced into Australia from South Africa). Since the start of the twentieth century outside contributions were limited to the Anglo-Arab, resulting in an animal used to good effect by the Indian and the Australian cavalry. Since 1932 the breed has gone into a progressive decline and has undergone many physical changes, consequently the present-day appearance is very different from that of the original Waler. Since 1971 the breed has been registered and controlled by a society set up to increase production of the modern version of the Waler, now known as the Australian Stock Horse and used in competitive sports as well as for polo.

85 BRUMBY

Breed Brumby.
Place of origin Australia.
Aptitudes Life in the wild state.
Qualities Hardy and unrefined.
Temperament Rebellious and intractable.
Conformation A horse of the mesomorphic type, whose height at the withers varies greatly, sometimes exceeding 15 hands (1·52 m); the coat may be of any color. The head is rather heavy, the neck and back short, the croup sloping, the shoulder straight, and the legs sturdy.
History This breed developed around the middle of the nineteenth century, when large numbers of horses were abandoned at the time of the gold rush in Australia. Once free these animals formed herds, reproducing prolifically and naturally. As with other breeds that have reverted to the wild, while freedom hardened them to all types of physical adversity and sharpened their cunning, it also caused their outward appearance to regress: they became smaller, and therefore needed less food, the primitive coat colors reappeared as camouflage, and the shoulder became straighter giving a less free-flowing action but greater speed, to allow the animal to take flight in moments of danger. The enormous increase in numbers of these horses eventually created problems in agriculture and organized culling became necessary, however, their remarkable cunning, heightened in the wild by the instinct for survival, made this a very difficult task. Since 1962 this relentless culling has brought the Brumby close to extinction.

HEAVY DRAFT BREEDS

Breed Belgian Brabant (Belgian Draft).
Place of origin Belgium.
Geographical distribution Europe, United States.
Aptitudes Slow heavy draft, farm work.
Qualities Strong and willing.
Temperament Docile and phlegmatic.
Conformation A pony of the brachymorphic type, standing 15·3–16·3 hands (1·60–1·70 m) at the withers, and weighing 1,760–2,200 lb (800–1,000 kg). The coat is generally roan. The head is small in relation to the body and squarish, with a prominent jaw, a straight or slightly concave profile, small ears and eyes, and a full forelock. The neck is short and muscular, very broad at the base, arched and well set-on; the withers are low, broad and muscular, the back broad and muscular, sometimes slightly hollow, the loins broad and short, the flanks well-developed, the croup muscular and rounded, the chest broad, muscular, full and deep, with well-rounded ribs, the abdomen well-developed, and the shoulder long and sloping and very muscular. The legs are short and sturdy, with broad, solid joints, the cannons are of a remarkable circumference, the pasterns short and feathered, the hoof large but flat, with rather soft horn.
History The origins of this breed are very distant, and are probably linked to the type of prehistoric horse that existed in the alluvial period of the Quaternary, whose fossilized remains have been found in the territory stretching from Liège to Dinant, along the right bank of the river Meuse. As the name of the breed suggests it has its origins in the Brabant area of Belgium. The characteristics of this breed were fixed at the beginning of the twentieth century, with contributions from three breeds of distinctive characteristics; the Gros de la Dendre, muscular with solid limbs, the Gris de Nivelles, with good conformation and a distinguished appearance, and the Colosses de la Mehaigne, with an energetic temperament. The Belgian Brabant has a sluggish constitution, which is noticeable from its docile, obedient, but generally over-impassive temperament. It is an early-developing and long-lived animal, strong and very willing with a slow but vigorous action. In times gone by it was exported to the United States, where it gave rise to the American Belgian, which is considerably taller in stature, standing 17–18·3 hands (1·72–1·90 m) at the withers. The Stud Book for the Belgian Brabant dates back to 1885 and is put out by the Societé Royale pour le Cheval de Trait Belge.

Note The **Belgian Ardennes** was once considered in some countries to be a division of the Belgian Brabant, however, it is now generally classed as a division of the French Ardennais, with which it shares the same features (see entry 92).
History The Belgian Ardennes comes originally from the Ardennes plateau, where the rigorous climate and very sparse pasture have toughened it making it hardy and frugal. Once highly regarded by Julius Caesar and Nero, in the eighteenth century it was ennobled by the introduction of Arab blood, and Napoleon himself made use of it for its exceptional endurance. The characteristics which distinguish the present-day type were established in the nineteenth century. The Belgian Ardennais now has its own genealogical book, run by the Societé Royale pour le Cheval de Trait Ardennais.

Breed Percheron (Trait Percheron).
Place of origin France (Le Perche region).
Geographical distribution France, Great Britain, United States, South America, South Africa, Australia, Japan.
Brand Letters SP on neck, initials of the Société Hippique Percheronne.
Aptitudes Draft and farm work.
Qualities Strong with good endurance.
Temperament Very quiet and docile, but energetic.
Conformation There are two varieties within the breed; the small variety, standing 14·3–16·1 hands (1·50–1·65 m) at the withers, and weighing 1,320–1,760 lb (600–800 kg), and the large, with a height of 16·1 to 17·3 hands (1·65–1·80 m), and a weight of 1,760–2,200 lb (800–1,000 kg). The most common coat is gray (typically dappled), while black and roan occur more rarely. The Percheron has a handsome head, quite long but harmonious in spite of its strong jaws, and small in relation to the size of the body, with a straight profile, broad forehead, well-proportioned ears, large, expressive eyes, and flared nostrils. The neck is short, broad and muscular, slightly arched, with a full mane and good general conformation; the withers are moderately prominent, the back sometimes slightly hollow, the loins full and rounded, the croup also wide and rounded (sometimes double-muscled), the chest broad and muscular, the girth wide and deep, the abdomen rounded, and the shoulder nicely sloping and muscular. The legs are short and robust, with broad joints, the thighs long and muscular, the pasterns short and lightly feathered, and the hoof large, with dark, tough horn.
History The breed originated in the region of Le Perche, and is probably descended from an ancient indigenous breed, said to descend from *Equus caballus sequanus*. During the course of its development the Percheron has benefited from infusions of Oriental blood, as is clearly shown by the elegant head and velvety coat. The first of these contributions was probably made in the eighth century A.D. using horses captured from the Saracens after their defeat at Poitiers, and the second in the Middle Ages by stallions imported by the Comte de Perche when he returned from the Crusades and expeditions into Spanish territory. There is also a certain proportion of Spanish blood deriving from stallions imported from Castille by the Comte de Rotrou. The small Percheron, also known as the Percheron Postier, is now virtually extinct, while the large version, used in the past for drawing omnibuses in towns and cities and for farm work, has survived the recent revolution in transport and agriculture. The breed's Stud Book goes back to 1883, and since 1966 also includes a series of local breeds which have their origin in the Percheron; these are the Trait Augeron (*trait* means draft), the Trait de la Loire, the Trait Berrichon, from the former province of Berry, the Trait du Maine, the Gros Trait Nivernais, the Trait de la Saône-et-Loire and the Trait Bourdonnais. The Stud Book is kept by the Société Hippique Percheronne, and since 1911 it has been restricted exclusively to horses that have both parents registered. In the United States the Percheron Society of America has existed since 1878 and has its own Stud Book. The Percheron was introduced into Great Britain from France during World War I, and its Stud Book has been strictly maintained since 1919; the Percheron had in fact been imported into Great Britain from the United States at the end of the nineteenth century proving particularly suited to drawing the London omnibus.

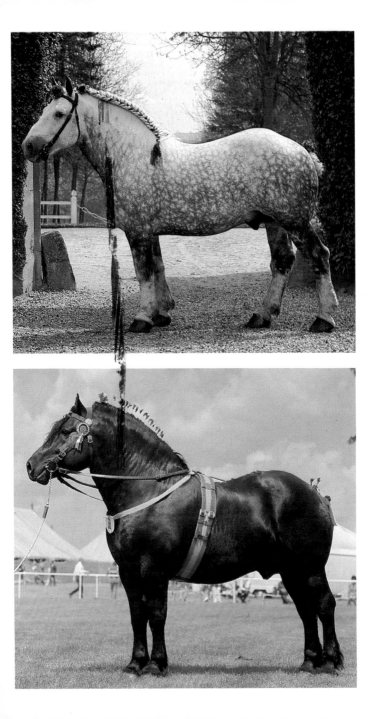

88 BOULONNAIS

Breed Boulonnais.
Place of origin France (northwest).
Brand Anchor on left side of neck.
Aptitudes Draft and farm work.
Qualities Strong, with good endurance.
Temperament Energetic and lively.
Conformation A horse of the brachymorphic type bred in two distinct versions, the small Boulonnais, standing 15·1–15·3 hands (1·55–1·60 m) at the withers, and weighing 1,210–1,430 lb (550–650 kg), and the large Boulonnais, at 15·3–16·3 hands (1·60–1·70 m), weighing 1,430–1,650 lb (650–750 kg). The usual coat is gray, often dappled, brown occurring occasionally. The head is small and square, with a straight profile, a broad forehead, well-proportioned ears, large, lively eyes, and flared nostrils. The neck is short and muscular, broad and quite arched; the withers are wide, low and muscular, the back short and straight, the croup slightly sloping, the chest full, with rounded ribs, the shoulder sloping and well-muscled. The legs are fairly short and robust, with broad joints, well-developed thighs, and a well-formed and solid hoof.
History This breed may descend from Numidian horses introduced into France by the Romans. These horses were later refined by crossing with the Arab, Andalusian and Mecklenburg. Another theory is that it derives from Hun horses abandoned by Attila. The small Boulonnais was once used to transport fish from the northern French ports, which explains the anchor in the breed's brand mark. The Stud Book goes back to 1886.

89 COMTOIS

Breed Comtois.
Place of origin France (Franche Comté).
Geographical distribution Eastern France.
Aptitudes Heavy draft, farm work.
Qualities Strong, good endurance, sure-footed.
Temperament Docile, active and willing.
Conformation A horse of the brachymorphic type, standing 14·1–15·1 hands (1·45–1·55 m) at the withers, and weighing 1,100–1,320 lb (500–600 kg), with some adult stallions reaching 1,760 lb (800 kg). The coat is chestnut or bay. The head is square, with a straight profile, broad forehead, a full forelock, and small, mobile ears. The neck is short and muscular, with a full mane; the withers are moderately well-defined, wide and muscular, the back straight, the croup wide and sloping, the tail set-on low, the chest wide and deep, the shoulder long and sloping. The legs, feathered in their lower parts, are slender in relation to the size of the body, but strong, sometimes showing a tendency to sickle hocks; the feet are solid.
History The breed is of very early origins and has probably been bred in the Franche Comté region since the sixth century. It almost totally descends from the Germanic horses imported into France by the Burgundians, a people coming from northern Germany, who in 411 A.D. founded the kingdom of Burgundy. It was used in the Middle Ages as a war horse. The Comtois is now bred in the mountainous region on the French-Swiss border. The Comtois has a quick lively action, unusual in a heavy draft breed, and is very sure-footed, enabling it to tackle steep and rugged mountain tracks and roads.

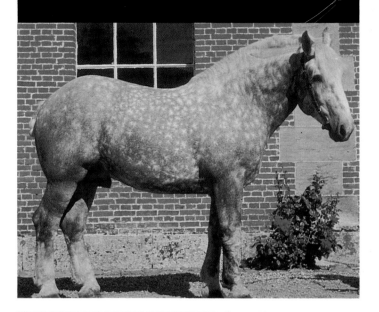

90 BRETON

Breed Breton.
Place of origin France (Brittany).
Geographical distribution Europe and Japan.
Brand A cross surmounting a splayed, upturned V.
Aptitudes Heavy draft, farm work.
Qualities Long endurance.
Temperament Energetic, lively.
Conformation A horse of the brachymorphic type, standing 15–16 hands (1·55–1·65 m) at the withers, and weighing 1,540–1,980 lb (700–900 kg); the breed is divided into three distinct morphological types: the Grand Breton, the medium or Postier-Breton, and the Corlay. The coat is generally chestnut, but bay, gray, roan or red roan also occur. The head is well-proportioned although the jaws are heavy, the profile is straight or slightly snub, the forehead broad, the ears short, and the nostrils flared. The neck is broad and muscular, arched, quite short, and well set-on; the withers are broad, muscular and not pronounced, the back is short and straight, the loins broad, the quarters sloping, full, and muscular; the chest is broad and muscular, like the shoulder, which is also long and sloping. The legs are short and powerful with broad, strong joints, the forearm and shin are well-muscled, the cannons sometimes slender but solid, the pasterns short and feathered, and the hoof well-formed and strong.
History According to some sources, the origins of this breed date back at least four thousand years, when it was brought into Europe by the Aryans, who were at that time emigrating from Asia. According to others, it stems from smaller horses that were bred and improved by Celtic warriors on the heathland and slopes of the Massif Armorique, before beginning their conquest of Great Britain. Perhaps the most glorious period in the long history of this horse came during the Middle Ages, when it was particularly sought after by military leaders for its comfortable and alluring gait, halfway between a brisk trot and an amble. Because of this gait, the Breton, which at the time measured only about 14 hands (1·40 m) at the withers, became known as the Bidet d'Allure or Bidet Breton. The Breton was influenced by blood it received from horses brought back from the Holy Land by the crusaders. Later, but still during the Middle Ages, there were two types of horse in Brittany, one heavier known as the "Sommier," which was used as a pack horse, and the other, lighter, called the "Roussin," which was used in wars and for long journeys. Subsequently, until 1800, they were crossed with other French heavy breeds from which, after the decisive introduction of the Norfolk Roadster and its descendant, the Hackney Trotter, the Postier-Breton was developed, so called because it was used for drawing mail coaches. The Grand Breton, which received contributions from the Ardennais, the Percheron and the Boulonnais, has today been practically reabsorbed by the medium size form which is now called the Fast Heavy Draft Breton. The Corlay, used as a riding horse and for light, fast draft work, was the lightest form of Breton and has now almost disappeared. The breed is controlled by the Syndicat des Éleveurs de Cheval Breton and its Stud Book was started in 1909. Only horses born in the four departments of Brittany, and in the Loire-Atlantique can be entered in this Stud Book. Registered foals are branded on the left side of the neck with the distinctive mark of the breed. In the past the Grand Breton was used to improve other heavy draft breeds.

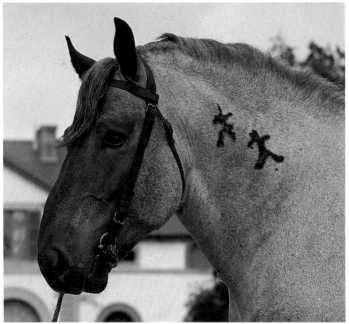

91 AUXOIS

Breed Auxois.
Place of origin France.
Geographical distribution France (Côte d'Or, Yonne, Saône-et-Loire).
Brand Letters TX on left side of neck.
Aptitudes Heavy draft and farm work.
Qualities Very strong, with excellent endurance.
Temperament Quiet, good-natured and willing.
Conformation A horse of the brachymorphic type, standing 15·1–16 hands (1·54–1·62 m) at the withers, and weighing 1,650–2,425 lb (750–1,100 kg); the coat may be bay or roan, occasionally chestnut or red roan. The head is light, the profile straight, the forehead broad, the ears small, and the expression of the eyes gentle. The neck is short, muscular and quite broad; the withers are not very pronounced, the back straight, the croup sloping, the tail set-on low, the chest wide and deep, and the shoulder long and sloping. The legs are slender in relation to the body, but sturdy.
History The breed dates back at least to the Middle Ages, and descends from the old Burgundian horse. Originally the horse was smaller in stature than it is today. In the nineteenth century the breed was influenced by the Percheron and the Boulonnais, and more recently also by the Ardennais and the Trait du Nord. Used in the past for drawing carriages and carts, with the advent of motorization, it became largely redundant, consequently suffering a drastic reduction in numbers. Today the breed is strictly controlled according to type and coat color by the Syndicat du Cheval de Trait Ardennais de l'Auxois based in Dijon, which has kept the Stud Book since 1913.

92 ARDENNAIS

Breed Ardennais (French Ardennais).
Place of origin France.
Aptitudes Heavy draft and farm work.
Qualities Strong, with good endurance.
Temperament Calm, but energetic.
Conformation A horse of the brachymorphic type, standing 15–16 hands (1·52–1·62 m) at the withers, and weighing 1,540–2,200 lb (700–1,000 kg); the coat may be bay, roan, chestnut, gray, red roan or palomino; brown and light chestnut are tolerated but black is excluded. The head is rather heavy, with pronounced jaws, a straight or snub profile, a broad face, small, pointed ears, large eyes, and flared nostrils. The neck is short, muscular and broad at the base; the withers are low, broad and muscular, the back short, broad and straight, the loins broad, the croup rounded, the chest broad and deep, and the shoulder muscular and sloping. The legs are sturdy, short and muscular, feathered, the joints strong, and the foot broad.
History The Ardennais is thought to be a descendant of a type of horse described by Julius Caesar in his *De Bello Gallico*, and may even be descended directly from the Solutré horse. At the time of the Romans this horse measured barely 14 hands (1·45 m). With the addition of Oriental blood at the time of Napoleon its stamina and endurance increased. In the course of the nineteenth century as a result of contributions by the Belgian Draft, it acquired its modern form and stature. Napoleon used these horses in his Russian campaign, and in fact the Russian Ardennais probably derives from horses left behind in the retreat. The breed has been registered since 1929.

93 TRAIT DU NORD

Breed Trait du Nord.
Place of origin France.
Geographical distribution France (northeast).
Aptitudes Heavy draft and farm work.
Qualities Strong and hardy.
Temperament Energetic, but quiet.
Conformation A horse of the brachymorphic type, standing 15·3–16·1 hands (1·60–1·65 m) at the withers, and weighing 1,320–1,760 lb (600–800 kg); the coat may be bay, roan or red roan. The head is heavy, with a straight profile, pronounced jaws and small ears and eyes. The neck is muscular, short and broad; the withers are wide and not very prominent, the back short and straight, the loins broad, the croup wide and muscular, slightly sloping, the chest wide and deep, the abdomen well-developed, and the shoulder muscular and nicely sloping. The legs are short and strong, well-muscled, feathered below the knee and hock, the joints are broad, and the foot well-formed; the natural stance is correct.
History The Trait du Nord inherits its heavy build and calm temperament from the Ardennais, the Belgian Draft and the Boulonnais, all of which contributed to its formation. However, in addition to these inherited characteristics, this breed also shows remarkable hardiness. Its strength is such that it is able to draw carts of exceptional weight, even over steep, hilly terrain. The Stud Book for the breed dates back to 1919. The horse is bred in the area around Lille, in the Pas-de-Calais, the Aisne, the Somme and Seine-et-Marne departments, but its numbers are on the decline.

---

94 POITEVIN

Breed Poitevin (Cheval du Poitou).
Place of origin France (Poitou).
Aptitudes Heavy draft and farm work.
Qualities Strong, good endurance.
Temperament Lethargic, well-balanced, but not very lively.
Conformation A horse of the brachymorphic type, standing 15–17 hands (1·53–1·73 m) at the withers, and weighing 1,540–1,980 lb (700–900 kg). The coat is usually bay, gray, black or palomino, it has a heavy head, with a straight or slightly convex profile, a full forelock, thick, large ears, and small, not very expressive eyes. The neck is short, broad and muscular, with a thick mane; the withers, also broad and muscular, are moderately pronounced, the back straight, broad and long, the loins broad, the croup fairly long and sloping, the tail full and flowing, the chest deep, the abdomen quite well-developed, and the shoulder sloping but not well-formed. The legs are rather thick and short, with some feather, broad joints, long cannons, and broad feet.
History This horse descends from horses of various extractions imported from the Netherlands, Norway and Denmark by the Dutch, who used them in land reclamation work in the region around Poitiers. These horses, crossed with local mares, produced the Poitevin breed also known as "Mulassier," meaning "mule breeder," because of its use in the production of mules. In the nineteen-fifties the Poitevin was in danger of extinction, but is currently enjoying a revival, thanks to a considerable demand from other countries. The genealogical register of the breed goes back to 1884.

95 SUFFOLK PUNCH

Breed Suffolk Punch.
Place of origin Great Britain.
Geographical distribution Europe.
Aptitudes Heavy draft.
Qualities Strong, frugal, early-maturing and long-lived.
Temperament Quiet and sociable.
Conformation A horse of the brachymorphic type, standing 15·3–16·1 hands (1–60–1·65 m) at the withers, and weighing 1,980–2,200 lb (900–1,000 kg); the coat is exclusively chestnut, with no white markings. The head is short and handsome in conformation, with a straight profile, broad forehead, and expressive eyes. The neck is short, broad at the base, muscular and arched; the withers are low and broad, the back short, wide and straight, the loins full and powerful, the croup broad and muscular, the chest wide, deep and muscular, and the shoulder long, sloping and well-muscled. The legs are rather short, but strong, well-muscled and almost without feathering, the joints broad, the cannons and pasterns short, the foot sound and well-formed.
History This native of the English county of Suffolk is certainly one of the descendants of the Great Horse. The breed dates back to 1506, and was created with contributions from the Norfolk Trotter and the Norfolk Cob, probably with a later contribution from the English Thoroughbred. The chestnut coat seems to derive from a small trotting stallion named Blakes Farmer (1760), who handed down his particular chestnut coloring to all his descendants. In the past the Suffolk was used for drawing brewers' drays, and omnibuses, and was also well-suited to farm work, and to drawing heavy artillery in times of war.

96 CLYDESDALE

Breed Clydesdale.
Place of origin Scotland (Lanarkshire).
Aptitudes Heavy draft and farm work.
Qualities Strong and hardy.
Temperament Calm and sociable.
Conformation A horse of the brachymorphic type, the females standing 16–16·1 hands (1·63–1·65 m) at the withers, and the males 16·1–17 hands (1·65–1·73 m); the weight varies from 1,540 to 2,200 lb (700–1,000 kg). The coat is generally bay, brown or black, chestnut and roan occurring more rarely. The head is not large, but has a broad face with a straight or convex profile, and flared nostrils. The neck is quite long, broad at the base, muscular and arched; the withers are pronounced, the back short and slightly hollow, the loins wide, the croup also wide, muscular and rather sloping, the chest wide and deep, and the shoulder sloping and muscular. The legs are robust and feathered, with strong joints; the pasterns are long, and the foot rounded; the hind legs are frequently cow-hocked.
History The Clydesdale originated in the eighteenth century, when a Lanarkshire farmer imported a stallion from Flanders. It is to this stallion that much of the credit for the subsequent development of the breed is due. Its official début under its present name was at the Glasgow Exhibition of 1826. The definitive characteristics of the breed were fixed at the beginning of the eighteenth century, following contributions from Flemish and Frisian stallions. It was used for coal haulage and farm work, and in Scotland eventually replaced the Shire as a carriage horse. The Stud Book was established in 1878.

97 SHIRE

Breed Shire.
Place of origin England.
Aptitudes Heavy draft and farm work.
Qualities Strong, with good endurance.
Temperament Docile and good-natured.
Conformation A horse of the brachymorphic type, generally standing 16·1–17·3 hands (1·65–1·80 m) at the withers, and weighing 1,760–2,200 lb (800–1,000 kg). The coat may be bay, brown, black, chestnut or gray, with frequent white markings. The head is small in relation to the body size, with pronounced jaws, a rather convex profile, a broad forehead, long ears, and large prominent eyes. The neck is quite long, arched and muscular; the withers are fairly wide and continue the line of the neck, the back short, the croup sloping but not too powerful, the chest broad and muscular, and the shoulder long and sloping. The legs are rather short, well-muscled and feathered below the knee and the hock, the joints are broad, the cannons fairly long, the pasterns short, and the foot sound.
History This breed is said to descend from the Great Horse, the medieval charger used in jousting, which derived from the most powerful draft horses in northern Europe, with some contributions of Oriental blood. The Stud Book for the breed was established in 1878. It was originally used as a carriage horse, then in agriculture and for drawing omnibuses. It is the world's tallest horse, in some cases reaching a height of 19 hands (1·92 m) and a weight of 2,640 lb (1,200 kg). The breed went into a decline in the nineteen-fifties, but since the centenary of the foundation of the stud book it has experienced a revival.

98 IRISH DRAFT

Breed Irish Draft.
Place of origin Ireland.
Geographical distribution Ireland.
Aptitudes Medium-heavy draft, farm work, riding horse.
Qualities Good jumper.
Temperament Quiet, but dynamic.
Conformation A horse of the meso-brachymorphic type, standing 15–17 hands (1·52–1·72 m) at the withers; the coat may be bay, brown, gray or chestnut. The head is well-proportioned, the profile straight, the forehead broad, and the ears pricked up. The neck is of average length and breadth; the withers are quite pronounced, the back long and straight, the croup fairly sloping, the tail well set-on, full and flowing, the chest wide and deep, the abdomen drawn in, the shoulder nicely sloping, massive and powerful. The legs are solid and well-muscled, with slight feathering, broad, tough joints, solid cannons and pasterns, and a broad, round foot.
History The origins of this breed are uncertain, although it is likely that it descends from the Connemara, with some Clydesdale importations in the nineteenth century. The Stud Book dates back to 1917, and is very strictly maintained. The female of the breed crossed with the English Thoroughbred produces the Irish Hunter, a first-rate sporting horse, which in show jumping is one of the best in the world. Despite its size and build the Irish Draft is itself a good natural jumper.

99 DØLE GUDBRANDSDAL

Breed Døle Gudbrandsdal.

Place of origin Norway.

Aptitudes Heavy draft, farm work, trotting racing.

Qualities Strong, good stamina.

Temperament Patient but energetic.

Conformation A horse of the meso-brachymorphic type, standing 14·1–15 hands (1·45–1·53 m) at the withers, and weighing 1,190–1,390 lb (540–630 kg). The coat is generally bay, brown, or black; gray and palomino occur more rarely. The head is heavy and rather square, with a full forelock, straight profile, long ears, and small eyes. The neck is rather short and muscular, with a full mane; the withers are broad and moderately pronounced, the back long and straight, the loins strong, the croup broad, muscular, and slightly sloping, the tail long and full, but set-on slightly low, and the chest wide and deep; the shoulder is strong and muscular, and nicely sloping. The legs are short and sturdy, well-muscled, with heavy feathering from the cannons down; the joints are broad and solid, the cannons short, the feet broad, with tough horn.

History In appearance this breed resembles the English Dales pony, and it therefore seems likely that both breeds share similar origins. The Døle has recently received contributions from the English Thoroughbred, and various trotting, or heavy draft breeds. A decisive influence was exerted by the stallion Odin, previously named Partisan, and reputedly a Norfolk Trotter, although considered by some to have been English Thoroughbred, and by the purebred Arab Mazarin, imported into Norway in 1934. The Døle contributed to the formation of the North Swedish Horse, to which it bears a remarkable resemblance. Because of its exceptional trotting ability, a lighter version is bred using a greater input of blood from trotting breeds to improve its racing performance. Since 1941, this version has been known as the Døle Trotter or Norwegian Trotter, and has its own Stud Book, carrying the letter "T," that of the working version having the letter "G." Between 1840 and 1860 three stallions played a particularly important rôle in the formation and development of the Døle Trotter. These were Veikle Balder, Toftebrun, and Dovre, the latter, registered in the breed records as G130, being the true foundation sire of this small trotting breed. The record kilometer time for the Døle Trotter is 1'21"6, established in 1986 by the five-year-old Alm Svarten.

The Døle Gudbrandsdal in its original version is used in Norway for hauling timber and general farm work.

100 NORTH SWEDISH HORSE

Breed North Swedish Horse (North Swedish Trotter – North-Hestur).
Place of origin Sweden.
Aptitudes Heavy draft, farm work, trotting racing.
Qualities Strong, hardy, good trotter, frugal, long-lived.
Temperament Calm but energetic.
Conformation A horse of the meso-brachymorphic type, standing 15–15·2 hands (1·53–1·56 m) at the withers; the coat may be bay, brown, black, chestnut or palomino. The head is of average size, but rather heavy, with a straight profile, broad forehead, long ears, and small but expressive eyes. The neck is fairly short, muscular and broad at the base, with a full, flowing mane; the withers are broad, low and muscular, the back long, wide and straight, the loins full, the croup wide and slightly sloping, the tail set-on low, with long, thick hair, the chest wide and deep, the abdomen large and rounded, and the shoulder muscular and sloping. The legs are rather short, with strong bone structure, broad joints, strong tendons, and tufts of feathering behind the fetlocks; the hoof is broad, rounded and solid.
History This horse has many points of similarity with the Døle Gudbrandsal. Its special aptitude for trotting has been increased by careful selection, thereby giving rise to the North Swedish Trotter or North-Hestur, which is a lighter version of the breed. The kilometer times recorded by this cold-blood trotter are, however, well above those of the true trotter racing breeds at around 1′30″. The Stud Book for the breed was established in 1924.

101 SWEDISH ARDENNES

Place of origin Sweden.
Geographical distribution Sweden
Aptitudes Heavy draft and farm work.
Qualities Strong, hardy, long-lived and frugal.
Temperament Quiet and docile, but energetic.
Conformation A horse of the brachymorphic type, standing 15–16 hands (1·52–1·62 m) at the withers; and weighing 1,100–1,540 lb (500–600 kg). The coat may be bay, brown, black or chestnut. The head is rather heavy, with a straight profile, broad forehead, full forelock, and small eyes. The neck is short and muscular, with a full mane; the withers are not very pronounced, broad and muscular, the back is short, the croup also muscular, rounded and often double, the chest wide and deep, and the shoulder sloping and muscular. The legs are short and sturdy, with light feathering, the joints broad and strong, and the foot broad and round, with tough horn.
History This breed was developed in the nineteenth century, with blood from the Belgian and French Ardennais, whose imprint may be seen both in the docile temperament and massive, compact appearance. The breed has suffered greatly as a result of the mechanization of road transport, but it continues to play a useful rôle in the transport of timber in mountainous regions.

102 JUTLAND

Breed Jutland.
Place of origin Denmark. -
Aptitudes Heavy draft and farm work.
Qualities Strong and willing.
Temperament Docile but energetic.
Conformation A horse of the brachymorphic type, standing 15–16·1 hands (1·52–1·65 m) at the withers, and weighing 1,430–1,760 lb (650–800 kg). The coat may be chestnut (most common), bay, gray or roan, frequently with white markings. The head is well-proportioned, with a slightly convex profile, small eyes, and erect ears. The neck is short, muscular and arched; the withers are low and wide, the back short and strong but often hollow, the loins wide and muscular, the croup full and slightly sloping, the chest wide and deep, and the shoulder quite straight and muscular. The legs are short and well-muscled, feathered, and fairly strong, with large feet.
History The ancient origins of this breed are unclear although the Romans would almost certainly have recognized it as the steed used by the Vikings. In the Middle Ages it was used for jousting, indicating it had a strong constitution capable of sustaining the weight of a knight in armor. In the nineteenth century it benefited from contributions of blood from the Suffolk Punch, the Cleveland Bay and more recently from the introduction of Ardennais blood. The Jutland bears a marked resemblance to another heavy draft breed, the Schleswig, which probably has similar origins. The development of both breeds was influenced by the Suffolk Punch stallion Oppenheim LXII, imported into Denmark in 1860.

103 DUTCH DRAFT

Breed Dutch Draft.
Place of origin Holland.
Geographical distribution Holland.
Aptitudes Heavy draft and farm work.
Qualities Strong and hardy.
Temperament Quiet, active, lively, willing.
Conformation A horse of the brachymorphic type standing approximately 16 hands (1·65 m) at the withers; the coat is generally chestnut, bay, or gray, in exceptional cases black. The head is well-formed, tending to be square, with a rather pronounced jaw, straight profile, broad forehead, short, straight ears, and smallish eyes, intelligent in expression. The neck is well set-on and powerful; the withers are low and broad, the back short and straight, the loins muscular, the croup sloping, the tail set-on low, the chest deep and roomy, and the shoulder long and nicely sloping. The legs are strong and muscular, well-feathered, with broad joints and solid hooves.
History The origins of this breed are recent, going back only to 1918, when crosses were made between Zeeland-type mares and Belgian Heavy Draft, then Belgian Ardennes stallions. Despite its massive size and build, this is an agile animal with a naturally easy action. It became quite popular, before motorization limited its usefulness for both transport and farm work.

104 SCHLESWIG HEAVY DRAFT

Breed Schleswig.
Place of origin West Germany.
Geographical distribution West Germany.
Aptitudes Heavy draft and farm work.
Qualities Hardy, willing.
Temperament Docile but energetic.
Conformation A horse of the brachymorphic type, standing 15·1–16·1 hands (1·55–1·65 m) at the withers, and weighing 1,430–1,760 lb (650–800 kg). The coat may be chestnut, bay or gray, with frequent white markings. The head is well-proportioned, with a slightly convex profile, pricked-up ears and small eyes. The neck is short, muscular and arched; the withers are low and broad, the back strong and short, but not always straight, the loins broad and muscular, the croup full and round, the chest wide and deep, and the shoulder rather straight and muscular. The legs are short and muscular, fairly solid and feathered; the hoof is large and rounded.
History This horse is derived from the Jutland, to which it bears a remarkable resemblance. In this breed, as in the Jutland, the contribution of the Suffolk Punch stallion Oppenheim LXII was decisive. The Stud Book for the breed was established in 1891. In the past the Schleswig was used for drawing omnibuses, as well as for various kinds of farm work and transport in general. Today, like many other similar breeds, it is much reduced in numbers due to the advent of motorization.

105 RHINELAND HEAVY DRAFT

Breed Rhineland Heavy Draft (Rhenish—German Cold-blood)
Place of origin West Germany.
Aptitudes Heavy draft and farm work.
Qualities Strong and hardy.
Temperament Calm, docile.
Conformation A horse of the brachymorphic type, standing 16–17 hands (1·62–1·72 m) at the withers, and weighing around 2,200 lb (1,000 kg). The coat may be chestnut or red roan (with tail and mane flaxen or black) or bay. The head is small but with pronounced jaws, a straight profile, a full forelock and small eyes. The neck is quite short, broad and muscular; the withers are low and broad, the back is short, wide and often slightly hollow, the loins broad and muscular, the flanks muscular and rounded, the croup also muscular and wide, slightly sloping, the chest wide and deep, the abdomen large and rounded, and the shoulder muscular and rather straight. The legs are short and well-muscled, feathered, with broad joints, short cannons and broad, tough feet.
History The origins of the breed go back to the second half of the nineteenth century and are closely linked to the Ardennais from which it is derived, though with an important contribution from the Belgian Heavy Draft. The Stud Book was established in 1876. Created as a breed for farm work and for use in transport generally, although it has retained its original characteristics it has acquired a variety of names, relating to the different regions in which it is reared, as is the case of the Niedersachsen Heavy Draft of Lower Saxony.

106 NORIKER

Breed Noriker (Pinzgauer—Oberlander—South German Cold-blood).
Place of origin Austria (Styria and Carinthia).
Geographical distribution Austria and Germany.
Aptitudes Heavy draft and farm work.
Qualities Strong and sensible.
Temperament Calm and docile.
Conformation A horse of the meso-brachymorphic type, standing 15·1–16·3 hands (1·55–1·70 m) at the withers, and weighing 1,540–1,980 lb (700–900 kg). The coat is generally bay, chestnut (sometimes roan), brown, black or spotted (Pinzgauer), while dappled and gray are rare. The head is slightly heavy, with a straight or slightly convex profile. The neck is short and muscular, with a flowing, wavy mane; the withers are broad and not very pronounced, the back long and slightly hollow, the croup wide and sloping, the tail set-on low, the chest wide and deep, and the shoulder straight and well-muscled. The legs are well-muscled, with broad, strong joints, the pasterns short, with feather, the foot broad, and the hoof well-formed.
History This breed was developed by the Romans in the province of Noricum (roughly present-day Styria and Carinthia). It was improved in the sixteenth century by the introduction of Neapolitan and Andalusian blood. The Stud Book was established in 1903. In the Tyrol the horse is known as the Pinzgauer and in Germany's Bavarian mountains a lighter version, the South German Cold-blood, has long been bred. In the nineteenth century some Norman, Cleveland, Holstein, Hungarian, Clydesdale and Oldenburg blood was added to establish this distinct branch of the Noriker.

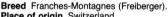

107 FRANCHES-MONTAGNES

Breed Franches-Montagnes (Freiberger).
Place of origin Switzerland.
Geographical distribution Switzerland, Italy and other European countries.
Aptitudes Light draft, farm work, riding horse.
Qualities Early-developing, steady, versatile.
Temperament Well-balanced, active, calm.
Conformation A horse of the mesomorphic type, standing 14·3–15.2 hands (1·50–1.58 m) at the withers, and weighing 1,210–1,430 lb (550–650 kg). The coat may be bay or chestnut only. The head is rather heavy, with pronounced jaws, a straight profile, a full forelock falling over a broad forehead, and small ears. The neck is muscular, arched, and broad at the base; the withers are broad and fairly pronounced, the back straight, the loins powerful, the croup slightly sloping, the chest wide and deep, the abdomen rounded, and the shoulder correctly sloping. The legs are short and clean, with good joints and tough hooves.
History This breed was developed around the end of the nineteenth century by crossing native Bernese Jura horses with the English Thoroughbred and the Anglo-Norman. Contributions were also made by the Ardennais, and by Arabs from the Hungarian stud farm at Babolna. There are two distinct strains within the breed, one more broadly built, with greater muscle development, the other lighter and better adapted to cross-country riding. Interbreeding of the two versions produces individual horses in which either tendency may predominate.

Breed Italian Heavy Draft.

Place of origin Italy.

Geographical distribution Italy.

Brand A shield containing a five-runged ladder applied both to the left thigh and to the left side of the neck.

Aptitudes Heavy draft and farm work.

Qualities Willing, hardy, fast for its size.

Temperament Good-natured, active, fairly highly-strung.

Conformation A horse of the brachymorphic type, the female standing 14·2–15·2 hands (1·48–1·58 m) at the withers, and the male 15–15·3 hands (1·52–1·60 m). The weight varies between 1,320 and 1,540 lb (600–700 kg). The coat may be chestnut (with lighter mane and tail), red roan or bay; no other colors are permitted. There may be white markings to the legs and other distinctive coat markings. The head is quite light, square and lean with a straight or slightly convex profile, a broad forehead, abundant forelock, quite small ears, large, lively eyes, flared nostrils, and a well-defined jaw. The neck, with a full mane, is short, muscular and very broad at the base; the withers are moderately pronounced. well-defined and muscular, the back short and straight, the loins powerful, flanks short and rounded, the croup (preferably double) rounded and sloping, the tail well set-on, the chest broad, deep and muscular, with well-rounded ribs, the abdomen well tucked up and the shoulder of a good length, fairly sloping and set close to the body. The legs are short, with some feather on the lower parts, the forearm is rather long, unlike the cannons, which are short, the pasterns are short and moderately sloping, the joints broad and generally rounded, and the hoof is smallish, well-proportioned and well-formed; the natural stance is correct.

History The breed dates back to 1860, when the stud farm at Ferrara, the Deposito Cavalli Stalloni, first began breeding native stallions from the Po Delta, subsequently introducing English Thoroughbred, Hackney and purebred Arab blood. In about 1900 efforts were made to increase the weight of the breed, using the Boulonnais, the Ardennais and the Norfolk-Breton. Horse breeding in Italy suffered badly during World War I and rigorous steps had to be taken to remedy the situation once hostilities were over. As a result Ardennais and Percheron stallions were introduced, however, it is to the Breton and a careful programme of crossbreeding, that the Italian Heavy Draft owes its distinctive characteristics.

109   SOKOLSKY

Breed Sokolsky.
Place of origin Poland.
Geographical distribution Poland.
Aptitudes Heavy draft and farm work.
Qualities Strong, good endurance, frugal, willing.
Temperament Docile and quiet.
Conformation A horse of the meso-brachymorphic type, standing 15–16 hands (1·53–1·63 m) at the withers; the coat is generally chestnut, but bay and brown are also found. The head is slightly heavy, with a straight profile, very upright, nicely proportioned ears, and expressive eyes. The neck is fairly long and muscular; the withers are pronounced, the back straight, the croup sloping, the chest and girth deep, and the shoulder nicely sloping. The legs are well-muscled and sturdy, with short cannons, strong tendons, and a broad, round hoof.
History The development of this breed, over the last hundred years, has been greatly influenced by the Norfolk, the Belgian Heavy Draft, the Belgian Ardennes and the Anglo-Norman. It is not an excessively heavy animal, and lends itself to various kinds of farm work.

110   MURAKOZ

Breed Murakoz.
Place of origin Hungary.
Geographical distribution Hungary, Poland, Yugoslavia.
Aptitudes Heavy draft and farm work.
Qualities Strong and frugal.
Temperament Docile but energetic.
Conformation A horse of the brachymorphic type, standing about 16 hands (1·63 m) at the withers; the coat may be chestnut (with mane, tail and feathering on the legs of a lighter color), bay, brown, black or gray. The head is rather long and heavy, with a somewhat convex profile, long ears, and gentle eyes. The neck is short and muscular, the withers low and broad, the back short, the croup sloping, the tail set-on low, the chest wide and deep, the abdomen tucked up, and the shoulder sloping and powerful. The legs are short and well-built, with good muscle and bone structure; the cannons and pasterns are short and feathered, and the hoof is well-proportioned and rounded.
History This breed was developed during the course of the twentieth century in the region around the River Mura in Hungary by crossing local mares with Belgian Ardennes, Percheron, Noriker, and also native stallions. During World War II the breed suffered serious losses, making it necessary to introduce new blood, again using Belgian Ardennes stallions. Well suited to heavy farm work, the Murakoz is now bred in two versions, one taller and heavier, the other smaller and lighter. It has generally good conformation, and is robust with a compact, powerful build from which it derives its great strength.

111   SOVIET HEAVY DRAFT

Place of origin Soviet Union.
Geographical distribution Soviet Union.
Aptitudes Heavy draft and farm work.
Qualities Hardy and strong.
Temperament Quiet but energetic.
Conformation A horse of the brachymorphic type, standing about 15·1 hands (1·55 m) at the withers, and weighing 1,430–1,720 lb (650–780 kg). The coat is usually chestnut, bay or roan. The head is well-proportioned but with pronounced jaws; the profile is straight or slightly convex, with a full forelock, well-proportioned, pointed ears, and gentle eyes. The neck is short and muscular, with a full mane; the withers are low and broad, the back and loins wide and strong, the croup muscular and sloping, the tail long and thick, the chest wide and deep, the abdomen rounded, and the shoulder straight and powerful. The legs are sturdy, with solid joints; the forearm is short, as are the legs, and the hoof is broad and rounded.
History The breed was developed between the end of the nineteenth century and the first decades of the twentieth, becoming firmly established in the nineteen-forties. It was originally formed by crossing native mares with imported Belgian and probably Percheron stallions. Despite its massive build, it has a sure and easy gait, both at the walk and the trot. In the Soviet Union it is the most commonly found horse of its type, and is used in the improvement of other heavy breeds, both on state-run farms and in the agricultural cooperatives known as kolkhozes.

112   RUSSIAN HEAVY DRAFT

Place of origin Soviet Union.
Geographical distribution Soviet Union (Ukraine).
Aptitudes Heavy draft and farm work.
Qualities Strong and hardy.
Temperament Quiet but energetic.
Conformation A horse of the brachymorphic type, standing 14·1–15 hands (1·44–1·52 m) at the withers; the coat may be chestnut, roan or bay. The head is of average size, with a straight or slightly convex profile, a broad forehead, with a full forelock, pointed ears, and lively eyes. The neck is of average length and muscular, and arched, with a full and flowing mane; the withers are low and broad, the back short and straight, the loins wide and muscular, the flanks powerful, the croup wide and slightly sloping, the tail long and full, the chest deep, with well-rounded ribs, the abdomen tucked up, and the shoulder sloping and powerful. The legs are short and lightly feathered, the thighs well-muscled, and the hooves tough.
History This breed has been gradually developing over the last hundred years by crossing local mares with stallions of various heavy draft breeds, such as the Swedish Ardennes, the Belgian Heavy Draft, and the Percheron, with some contributions also from the Orlov. Specifically created for agricultural work, this horse displays a powerful and harmonious conformation. It is robust and lively, and has a supple, flowing action both at the walk and at the trot.

113 VLADIMIR HEAVY DRAFT

Breed Vladimir Heavy Draft.
Place of origin Soviet Union (Vladimir).
Geographical distribution Soviet Union (Vladimir).
Aptitudes Heavy draft and farm work.
Qualities Very vigorous.
Temperament Energetic, vigorous, willing.
Conformation A horse of the brachymorphic type, standing 15·1–16 hands (1·55–1·63 m) at the withers, and weighing 1,500–1,675 lb (680–760 kg). The coat may be chestnut, bay, brown, or black; white markings are frequent. The head is of average size, but with a heavy jawline, the profile is often convex, and the ears pricked. The neck is of average length and muscular, broad at the base and arched; the withers are quite high and long, the back short, strong and straight, the loins short and strong, the croup wide and sloping, the chest wide and deep, the abdomen tucked up, and the shoulder sloping and powerful. The legs are solid and short, quite well-feathered, the thigh muscular, and the hoof broad and rounded.
History The breed was created in the second half of the nineteenth century by crossing various heavy draft breeds, such as the Ardennais, the Suffolk Punch, the Cleveland Bay, the Clydesdale and the Shire. After the Russian Revolution a policy of interbreeding was undertaken and there was no further recourse to outside contributions. In 1946 the breed was registered under its present name. Selection is strictly controlled by means of arduous practical trials.

114 LITHUANIAN HEAVY DRAFT

Breed Lithuanian Heavy Draft.
Place of origin Soviet Union (Lithuania).
Geographical distribution Soviet Union.
Aptitudes Heavy draft and farm work.
Qualities Strong and hardy.
Temperament Quiet.
Conformation A horse of the meso-brachymorphic type, standing 15 to 16 hands (1·52–1·63 m) at the withers; the coat may be chestnut, bay, black, gray or roan. The head is well-proportioned, but with a rather heavy jaw, a straight profile, full forelock, and large ears. The neck is quite short and muscular, arched, with a full mane; the withers are broad and moderately pronounced, the back straight, the croup rounded, the tail well set-on, full and long, the chest wide, deep, muscular, and quite massive. The legs are short, muscular and solid, with broad, strong joints, long cannons, and a broad, well-formed hoof.
History This breed derives from the local Zhmud horse, with contributions from the Finnish horse and the Swedish Ardennes. Its formation began at the end of the nineteenth century, but has been controlled and registered only since 1963. Selection is carried out by means of practical tests, to which all stallions destined for breeding are submitted. The horse is similar to the Latvian Harness Horse, both in its origins and its build. Both breeds have an attractive action at both the walk and the trot, and still play an important part in the agricultural economy of their respective regions.

PONIES

115 TARPAN

Breed Tarpan (*Equus przewalskii gmelini*).
Place of origin Poland.
Aptitudes Life in the wild.
Qualities Resistant to harshness of climate; a prolific breeder.
Temperament Courageous, independent, intractable.
Conformation A pony of the mesomorphic type, standing about 13 hands (1·30 m) at the withers; the coat may be mouse dun, yellow dun, or palomino, with a black eel stripe down the center of the back, a black mane and tail and black or zebra-marked legs. The head is rather heavy, with a slightly convex profile, long ears, pointing forward and slightly to the side, small, almond-shaped eyes, and a thick forelock. The neck is short and thick, with a full mane; the withers are not prominent, the back is straight and long, the croup sloping, the tail well set-on and flowing, the chest deep, and the shoulder nicely sloping. The legs are slender but strong.
History The Tarpan is regarded as the progenitor of all lightly-built breeds now in existence, although it is itself now extinct. The last member of the breed living in the wild died in 1879 in a desperate attempt to avoid capture, and the last Tarpan in captivity died in Munich zoo in 1887. It was a difficult pony to tame for use in agriculture. There were two distinct types of Tarpan, one living on the steppes, and the other in forested areas. Both strains lived in the wild in Eastern Europe, from Poland to the Ukraine. In an attempt to restore the breed the Polish government commandeered all horses displaying features similar to those of the Tarpan, and put them into the forests of Popielno and Bialowieza. The result was the type of horse illustrated in the photograph.

116 HUCUL

Breed Hucul (Carpathian pony).
Place of origin Poland (Carpathians).
Geographical distribution Poland, Great Britain.
Aptitudes Light draft, pack horse, farm work.
Qualities Frugal, willing, good endurance.
Temperament Calm, docile.
Conformation A horse of the mesomorphic type, attractive in appearance and solidly built, standing 12–13 hands (1·23–1·33 m) at the withers. The most common coats are bay, palomino, dun, mouse dun and, more rarely, gray. The head is well-proportioned, with a slightly snub profile, full forelock, small, pointed ears, small eyes, and flared nostrils. The neck is well-proportioned and of a nice length, with a long, full mane; the withers are quite pronounced, the back straight and long, the flanks well-formed, the croup sloping, the tail set-on low, long and flowing, the chest wide and deep, and the shoulder slightly sloping. The legs are well-muscled, with solid joints, long cannons, and small feet, with tough horn.
History Like the Konik, which it resembles, this pony is descended from the Tarpan. In fairly recent times it has also received contributions of Arab blood. Formal breeding of this pony dates back to the nineteenth century, and has been developing in various centers, one of which is Great Britain. It is an undemanding, hardy animal, which can be put to many uses; it is particularly well-suited to mountainous regions.

117 KONIK

Breed Konik.
Place of origin Poland.
Geographical distribution Poland.
Aptitudes Farm work.
Qualities Frugal, long-lived.
Temperament Quiet and willing, but sometimes independent, liking its freedom, and therefore difficult to handle.
Conformation A pony of the mesomorphic type, standing 12·3–13·3 hands (1·30–1·40 m) at the withers; the coat is generally mouse dun or palomino (with darker-colored or black eel stripe, mane and tail, and occasional zebra markings on the legs), gray and bay, the latter with bluish highlights. The head is rather heavy and not well set-on, with a slightly convex profile, small, pointed ears, full forelock, and flared nostrils. The neck is rather long, but broad and muscular, with a long, full mane; the withers are moderately pronounced, the back short and straight, the loins well set-on, the croup sloping, the tail set-on low but full and flowing, the chest wide and deep, and the shoulder very sloping. The legs are sturdy, with broad, clean joints, strong tendons, and a small, well-formed hoof.
History This is certainly a descendant of the Tarpan, though its appearance has been refined by probable infusions of Arab blood. The Konik, whose name means "little horse" in Polish, has inherited the hardiness and frugality of the Tarpan, and because of its qualities has been used in the improvement of other Polish and Russian horse and pony breeds.

118 ASIATIC WILD HORSE

Breed Asiatic Wild Horse, or Mongolian Wild Horse (*Equus przewalskii* Poliakov).
Place of origin Mongolia.
Aptitudes Life in the wild.
Qualities Strong and hardy.
Temperament Courageous, energetic.
Conformation A pony of the mesomorphic type, standing 12–14 hands (1·23–1·43 m) at the withers; the coat may be palomino, or yellow dun, with dark legs, mane and tail; zebra markings on the legs are frequent. The head is large and heavy, with a straight profile, broad forehead, long ears, and small, almond-shaped eyes; there are mealy markings on the muzzle. The neck is broad and quite short, with a short, bristly mane; the withers are not prominent, the back is straight and rather long, the loins are strong, the croup sloping, the tail set-on low, the chest deep, and the shoulder straight. The legs are short and sturdy, with short pasterns, and a very elongated hoof.
History This pony, discovered in 1881 by Colonel Poliakov, originated in the Daqin Shan Mountains ("mountains of the yellow horse") at the edge of the Gobi desert where it lived until recently. It is now extinct in the wild, although there are still a few living in captivity and there are plans to try and establish some as wild herds in their original habitat. These horses, were once the steeds of the Huns and the Chinese and it is from them that the majority of present-day breeds are descended.

119 MONGOLIAN

Breed Mongolian.
Place of origin Mongolia.
Aptitudes Riding pony, pack pony, farm work, light draft.
Qualities Hardy, frugal.
Temperament Tolerant, active.
Conformation A pony of the mesomorphic type, standing 12–14 hands (1·23–1·42 m) at the withers; the coat may be brown, black, mouse dun or palomino. The head is heavy, with a straight profile, a full forelock, short ears, and small almond-shaped eyes. The neck is quite short and thick, with a full, flowing mane; the withers are short and low, the back strong, short and straight, the loins also short, the croup long and sloping, the tail full and long, the chest deep, and the shoulder fairly sloping and muscular. The legs are sturdy, with solid bone structure, and well-muscled; the joints are broad, and the hoof rounded and hard.
History This is one of the oldest breeds, and has had a great influence on most Asiatic breeds. The Mongols, a notoriously warlike people, used these horses on their raids into neighboring territories, which resulted in the breed becoming widely diffused in the countries they invaded. Hence, for example, the similarity between the Mongolian and Tibetan ponies. The breed, which is still reared by the nomadic tribes of Mongolia, is found in a number of different types, that have developed according to differing environmental factors, and differing degrees of contact with other breeds. The most sought-after variety is the Wuchumutsin, reared in the more fertile, richly-pastured regions.

120 MANIPURI

Breed Manipuri.
Place of origin India (Assam, Manipur).
Aptitudes Riding pony.
Qualities Fast, hardy.
Temperament Docile but energetic.
Conformation A pony of the mesomorphic type, standing 11–13 hands (1·12–1·32 m) at the withers; the coat is generally bay, brown, gray or chestnut. The head is light and well-proportioned, with a straight profile, very alert ears, and almond-shaped eyes. The neck is well-formed, with a full mane; the withers are moderately pronounced, the back straight, the croup slightly sloping, the tail well set-on, the chest deep, the shoulder nicely sloping. The legs are well-built and sturdy, and the foot well-proportioned, with tough horn.
History This ancient breed descends from the Asiatic wild horse and the Arab and was probably introduced into India by invading Tartar tribes, who are also thought to have brought with them the game of polo. Although polo was widespread in Asia it was virtually unknown to Europeans until the mid nineteenth century when British colonials in India watched it for the first time, played with Manipuri ponies. The Manipuri is still used for polo in India, but in Europe and America the horses used as polo ponies are larger, faster and quicker off the mark. The Manipuri has a fairly elegant appearance, which it inherits from its Arab forebears.

121 SPITI

Breed Spiti.
Place of origin India (Himalayas).
Geographical distribution India (Himalayas).
Aptitudes Pack pony.
Qualities Strong and hardy.
Temperament Capricious.
Conformation A pony of the mesomorphic type, standing approximately 12 hands (1·22 m) at the withers; the coat is generally gray. The head is rather heavy, with a straight profile, a full forelock and small ears and eyes. The neck is short, with a full and flowing mane; the withers are low, the back short, the loins strong, the croup slightly sloping, the tail long and full, the chest deep, and the shoulder sloping and muscular. The legs are short and sturdy, well-muscled and with good bone structure, the joints broad and strong, and the foot rounded with tough horn.
History In appearance this pony closely resembles the Tibetan pony, which would appear to have similar origins, a theory that is supported by the fact that both breeds are from the Himalayas. The Spiti is a sturdy, vigorous mountain pony with fairly refined features, ill-suited to lowland conditions, where it is intolerant of the warm, humid climate. Its domain is the Himalayan mountains, where it fulfills an indispensable rôle as a pack animal. The Bhutia is a larger, more thickset version of the Spiti and is otherwise similar in origins, aptitudes, form, and shape.

122 KATHIAWARI AND MARWARI

Breed Kathiawari and Marwari.
Place of origin India (Kathiawari and Marwari).
Geographical distribution India (Kathiawari and Marwari).
Aptitudes Riding pony, pack pony, farm work, light draft.
Qualities Hardy, frugal.
Temperament Tenacious, but unpredictable.
Conformation Ponies of the meso-dolichomorphic type, of a good size, standing approximately 14 hands (1·43 m) at the withers. The usual coats are bay, brown, gray, chestnut, palomino, piebald and skewbald. The head is of average size, with a straight profile and pointed ears, the tips of which turn inward. The neck is slender and of average length; the withers are pronounced, the back long and straight, the croup sloping, the chest deep, and the shoulder rather straight. The legs are slender and graceful, the natural stance correct, the foot small and well-formed.
History These two breeds are generally classed together as they are almost identical. They both descend from native ponies crossed with Arab horses that appear to have swum ashore from a cargo ship wrecked on the west coast of India; these horses mated in total liberty with small, indigenous pony breeds, which were hardy and frugal, only about 13 hands (1·32 m) high and had poor conformation. The Arab influence improved the appearance of these ponies, without taking away their hardiness and frugality.

123 TIBETAN

Breed Tibetan (Nanfan).
Place of origin Tibet.
Geographical distribution Tibet.
Aptitudes Riding pony, pack pony, farm work.
Qualities Strong, hardy.
Temperament Docile, but energetic and lively.
Conformation A pony of the mesomorphic type, standing approximately 12·1 hands (1·24 m) at the withers; the coat may be almost any color, but the most common is yellow dun. The head is not large, but has rather pronounced jaws, with a straight profile, a broad forehead, and a full forelock; the ears are small and pointed, the eyes small and almond-shaped. The neck is short and muscular, with a full, long mane; the withers are not very pronounced, the back short, the loins wide and strong, the croup rounded, the tail full and flowing, the chest deep, and the shoulder rather straight. The legs are short and sturdy, well-built and muscular, with good joints and well-formed hooves.
History This pony probably derives from the Mongolian and Chinese ponies, and is related to the Bhutia and the Spiti, which it resembles in appearance. It is a fairly robust, vigorous animal, well-suited to a variety of tasks.

124 CASPIAN

Breed Caspian.
Place of origin Iran.
Aptitudes Riding pony.
Qualities Strong with good endurance, good jumper.
Temperament Docile, quiet.
Conformation A pony of the meso-dolichomorphic type, standing 9·2–11·2 hands (0·96–1·16 m) at the withers; according to the British Caspian Society the height should be between 10·2 and 12 hands (1·06–1·22 m). The coat may be chestnut, bay or gray with, in exceptional cases, white markings on the head and legs. The head is small, with a straight profile, tapering muzzle, full forelock, short ears, large eyes, and flared nostrils. The neck is muscular, slightly arched, with a long, full mane; the withers are quite pronounced, the back short and straight, the croup slightly sloping, the tail full and well set-on, the chest deep, and the shoulder nicely sloping. The legs are sturdy and well-built, with good bones and joints, clearly defined tendons, and a small, strong hoof.
History The breed apparently goes back to 3000 B.C., and was already domesticated by the ancient peoples of Mesopotamia. Its attractive appearance and superb bearing suggest that it may be a progenitor of the Arab horse. The breed was thought to have become extinct in the tenth century, but in 1965 a number of specimens were found in the Elburz mountains and on the shores of the Caspian Sea. Interestingly, finds unearthed near Kermanshah in Iran show similarities in size and skeletal structure to the ancient miniature horse of Mesopotamia.

125 CHINESE

Breed Chinese.
Place of origin China.
Geographical distribution China.
Aptitudes Riding and pack pony, farm work.
Qualities Hardy and strong; suitable for mountainous regions.
Temperament Quite rebellious.
Conformation A pony of the mesomorphic type, standing 12–13 hands (1·22–1·32 m) at the withers; the coat is usually yellow dun, but other colors may occur. The head is small, with a straight profile, a full, but shaggy forelock, small ears, and small, slanting eyes. The neck is short, with a thick, shaggy mane; the withers are rather low, the back straight, the croup slightly sloping, the chest deep, and the shoulder straight. The legs are sturdy.
History There is a strong resemblance between this pony and other pony breeds scattered throughout the Far East, which have similar origins. The Chinese pony certainly derives from the Asiatic wild horse. The frequent appearance and certain "primitive" characteristics, such as the dun coat, zebra markings on the legs, and the eel stripe, indicate the limited evolutionary level reached.

126 TIMOR

Breed Timor
Place of origin Indonesia (island of Timor).
Geographical distribution Indonesia (island of Timor).
Aptitudes Riding pony, farm work, light draft.
Qualities Good endurance, nimble.
Temperament Docile and willing.
Conformation A pony of the mesomorphic type, standing 9–10·3 hands (0·92–1·10 m) at the withers; the coat may be bay, brown, or black. The head is quite large and heavy, with a straight profile, short ears, and flared nostrils. The neck is short and muscular, broad at the base; the withers are quite pronounced, the back short, the croup slightly sloping, the chest deep, and the shoulder quite straight. The legs are sturdy, and the foot small, with tough horn.
History The similarity in appearance between this pony and the Greek Skyros pony may be explained by the fact that both breeds come from islands and have therefore been subjected to strict isolation, which has undoubtedly contributed to the conservation of the "primitive" type. Its origins must be similar to those of other Asiatic ponies. Although not a particularly attractive breed, with relatively poor conformation, the Timor plays a valuable rôle on the island, both as a riding pony and for light farm work.

127 BALI

Breed Bali.
Place of origin Indonesia (Bali).
Geographical distribution Indonesia (Bali)
Aptitudes Riding and pack pony.
Qualities Strong, frugal.
Temperament Docile, quiet.
Conformation A pony of the mesomorphic type, standing 12–13 hands (1·21–1·33 m) at the withers; the coat is generally dun with a black eel stripe, black mane and tail, and dark points. The head is rather large, with a straight profile, small ears, and slanting eyes. The neck is nicely proportioned, with a bristly, upright mane; the withers are quite low, the back short and straight, the croup slightly sloping, the chest deep, and the shoulder slightly sloping. The legs are sturdy.
History This pony does not differ greatly from other Indonesian ponies. Its origins are certainly distant, as shown by its coat and primitive eel stripe, and its upright mane is reminiscent of the Asiatic wild horse, from which it probably descends. In Bali it is used as a pack pony to transport coral for the building trade, and on the beaches to give rides to the many tourists attracted to the country by its natural beauty.

---

128 SANDALWOOD

Breed Sandalwood.
Place of origin Indonesia (Sumba and Sumbawa).
Geographical distribution Indonesia (Sumba and Sumbawa).
Aptitudes Riding and pack pony, light draft, farm work.
Qualities Endurance, speed.
Temperament Quiet but energetic.
Conformation A pony of the mesomorphic type, standing 12–13 hands (1·23–1·33 m) at the withers; the coat may be any color. The head is nicely proportioned, rather square, with a straight profile, a full forelock falling over its forehead, small, very alert ears, and expressive eyes. The neck is in proportion, with a full mane; the withers are slightly prominent, the back long and straight, the croup slightly sloping, the chest well-developed, and the shoulder nicely sloping. The legs are good and hard.
History The breed is so named after one of Indonesia's principal exports: sandalwood. In appearance it resembles the Batak, probably because of the influence of Arab blood on both breeds. Gifted with great endurance, and surprisingly fast for its size, it is used on the island in local bareback races over distances of 2½–3 miles (4–5 km).

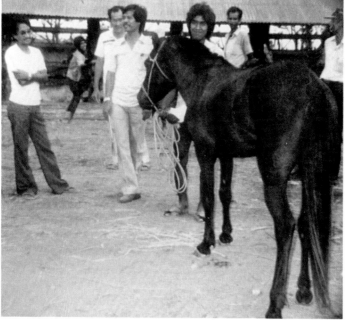

129 JAVA

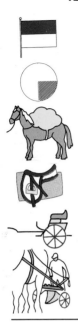

Breed Java.
Place of origin Indonesia (Java).
Geographical distribution Indonesia (Java).
Aptitudes Riding and pack pony, light draft, farm work.
Qualities Strong, hardy.
Temperament Docile, willing.
Conformation A pony of the meso-dolichomorphic type, standing about 12 hands (1·23 m) at the withers; the coat may be any color. The head is heavy, with a straight profile. The neck is short and muscular, with a thick mane; the withers are quite pronounced, the back straight and long, the croup slightly sloping, the chest well-developed, and the shoulder slightly sloping. The legs are long and well-muscled.
History In appearance this pony bears a close resemblance to the Timor, although it has slightly better conformation, a more sloping shoulder and is taller and stronger. The origins of these two breeds are presumably similar, but the Java has been more decisively influenced by the Arab. In Java it is used for pulling the "sados," a type of two-wheeled taxi used for transporting people and goods around the island. Despite the Arab influence it is not a particularly attractive breed, but this is compensated for by its sturdiness and willing nature.

130 BATAK

Breed Batak.
Place of origin Indonesia (Sumatra).
Geographical distribution Indonesia (Sumatra).
Aptitudes Riding pony.
Qualities Frugal.
Temperament Docile, lively.
Conformation A pony of the meso-dolichomorphic type, standing 12–13 hands (1·21–1·33 m) at the withers. The coat may be any color. The head is light, with a slightly convex profile, and a full forelock. The neck is arched and well-shaped; the withers are quite prominent, the back short, the croup slightly sloping, the tail well set-on, the chest deep, and the shoulder nicely sloping. The legs are sturdy, slender and well-muscled, and the foot well-formed.
History This pony, which originates from the island of Sumatra, is the most highly regarded of all the Indonesian breeds and results from crosses between Arab stallions and selected mares from different breeds on other islands. The best stallions are then sent back to these other islands to improve local breeds. In Sumatra another breed is also reared, called the Gayoe, which is less lively in temperament, and heavier than the Batak.

131 FJORD

Breed Fjord (Westlands Pony).
Place of origin Norway.
Aptitudes Riding and pack pony, light draft, farm work.
Qualities Strong, tireless, frugal.
Temperament Gentle but stubborn.
Conformation A fairly large pony of the mesomorphic type, standing 13–14·1 hands (1·32–1·44 m) at the withers. The characteristic coat is light dun, with a black and silver mane, an extensive eel stripe, and possible zebra markings on the legs. The head is small, but with pronounced jaws, a straight or slightly concave profile, broad forehead, small ears, set well apart, large, expressive eyes, and flared nostrils. The neck is short and muscular, with an upright mane; the withers are low, the back not too long and often slightly hollow, the loins strong, the croup rather sloping, the tail long and full, the chest full and deep, and the shoulder very sloping and muscular. The legs are sturdy and muscular, with broad, clean joints, clearly defined tendons, light feather behind the fetlocks, pasterns long, and the foot long with tough horn.
History This ancient breed has succeeded in retaining the "primitive" characteristics of its forebears from the Ice Age, as the dun coat, eel stripe, and zebra markings on the legs clearly show. The Vikings used these ponies as mounts in times of war as is proved by cave and rock paintings. It is thought that all present-day heavy draft breeds in western Europe are descended from this pony. The breed has withstood attempts to introduce foreign blood and is now reared as a purebred. In its own country it is used in small-scale harness trotting races.

132 NORTHLANDS

Breed Northlands.
Place of origin Norway.
Aptitudes Riding pony, light draft.
Qualities Strong, frugal.
Temperament Quiet but energetic.
Conformation An attractive-looking pony of the mesomorphic type, standing about 13 hands (1·32 m) at the withers. The coat is commonly chestnut, bay, brown or gray. The head is well-proportioned, with a straight profile, full forelock, small, upright ears, and eyes not too close together. The neck is quite short with a full mane; the withers are not too high, the back long and straight, the croup rounded, the tail long, full, and well set-on, the chest wide and deep, and the shoulder muscular and nicely sloping. The legs are sturdy and well-muscled, with broad, clean joints, and a strong, well-proportioned hoof.
History The origins of this pony can be traced back to the northern pony type descended from the Asiatic wild horse and the Tarpan, which were also the forebears of the Baltic pony (Konik) and the Celtic ponies (Icelandic, Shetland, and Exmoor). Until the second decade of the twentieth century the Northlands was bred by individual farmers in the traditional way, without following any particular selection process. After World War I some breeders made a conspicuous effort to regulate the standard of breeding. In spite of such initiatives, however, the number of ponies registered in 1944 had fallen to only forty-three. Since than the breed has seen a revival, for which much of the credit is due to the stallion Rimfakse.

133 ICELANDIC PONY

Breed Icelandic Pony.
Place of origin Iceland.
Aptitudes Riding and pack pony, light draft.
Qualities Hardy, frugal, strong, good pacer.
Temperament Quiet, friendly, independent.
Conformation A pony of the mesomorphic type, standing 12–13 hands (1·21–1·34 m) at the withers, and weighing 840–900 lb (380–410 kg). The coat may be almost any color, from chestnut to dun, bay, brown, black, gray, mouse dun, and even piebald and skewbald. The head is well-proportioned, but with slightly pronounced jaws, the profile is straight, the forehead wide, with a full forelock, the ears small, the eyes lively, and the nostrils flared. The neck is short and muscular, quite broad at the base, with a full but coarse mane; the withers are quite low and broad, the back long but sometimes slightly hollow, the croup short and broad, muscular and slightly sloping, the tail long and full but coarse and set-on low; the chest is deep, and the shoulder nicely sloping and muscular. The legs are short and strong, with broad, clean joints, relatively long cannons, short pasterns, and a strong hoof.
History This pony was probably brought to Iceland by the Norwegians in the ninth century, but following the arrival there of the Celts from Ireland and Scotland it was crossed with other breeds, such as the Shetland, the Highland, and the Connemara. At present it is bred in strict purity. A sure-footed pony, it treads fearlessly over the most difficult terrain. It has a fast comfortable, ambling gait called the "tölt," which enables it to cover a lot of ground.

134 GOTLAND

Breed Gotland (Skogsruss)
Place of origin Sweden (Gotland Islands)
Aptitudes Riding pony, light draft.
Qualities Strong, hardy, frugal, good trotting pony.
Temperament Alert, intelligent, but stubborn.
Conformation An attractive pony of the mesomorphic type, with elegant features; it stands 12–13·1 hands (1.22–1·34 m) at the withers and weighs 400–440 lb (180–220 kg). The most common coats are bay, brown, black, chestnut, gray, dun, palomino and mouse dun. The head is small, with a straight profile, small, broad ears, lively eyes, and flared nostrils. The neck is quite short and muscular, with a full mane; the withers are prominent, the back quite long and straight, but slightly weak, the croup sloping, the tail full and flowing, the chest deep, and the shoulder well-muscled and nicely sloping. The legs are strong and well-muscled, with solid joints, clearly defined tendons, long cannons, a strong hoof.
History The Gotland has characteristics in common with the Konik and the Hucul suggesting that these three breeds have similar origins. It has existed from prehistoric times on the island of Gotland in the Baltic Sea. In the nineteenth century two Oriental stallions were imported into Gotland, giving the pony its elegant and harmonious comformation. Since 1954 the breed has been protected and allowed to breed more or less in the wild state in the Löjsta forest. It is sometimes called "Skogsruss," meaning "little horse of the woods," and "little goat" because of its sure-footedness.

135 DARTMOOR

Breed Dartmoor.
Place of origin Great Britain (Dartmoor, Devon).
Aptitudes Riding pony.
Qualities Strong, hardy.
Temperament Quiet and sensitive.
Conformation A pony of the mesomorphic type with a distinguished, well-balanced appearance; the maximum height permitted for the breed is 12·2 hands (1·27 m). The most common coats are bay, brown, black and gray, while chestnut is more rare; piebald and skewbald are not admitted, and extensive white markings discouraged. The head is small, with a straight profile, broad forehead, an abundant forelock, small, pricked ears, and rather small eyes. The neck is well-proportioned and muscular, with a full mane; the withers are quite prominent, the back generally good, the loins broad, the croup wide and slightly sloping, the tail well set-on, long and full, the chest wide and deep, and the shoulder long and sloping. The legs are slender but sturdy, well-muscled, with clean joints, clearly defined tendons, and a well-formed foot, with tough horn.
History This very ancient breed of pony lives wild on Dartmoor, a rugged moorland area in southwest Devon. The purity of the breed was placed in jeopardy by the introduction into the region of Shetland stallions, but since 1899 the Dartmoor Pony Society has kept a strictly controlled register to ensure the breed's authenticity. Its good conformation and attractive appearance are probably due to the influence of the English Thoroughbred, which was used in the past to improve the breed. Its reliable nature makes it an ideal mount for young children.

136 NEW FOREST

Breed New Forest.
Place of origin Great Britain (New Forest).
Aptitudes Riding pony.
Qualities Willing.
Temperament Docile.
Conformation A well-built pony of the mesomorphic type, standing 12–14 hands (1·22–1·44 m) at the withers. All coat colors are permitted, except piebald and skewbald; the most common colors are bay and brown; white markings on the head and legs are admitted. The head is well-proportioned, with a straight profile, a broad forehead, with a full forelock, nicely proportioned ears, small eyes, and flared nostrils. The neck, not too long and muscular, has a long, full mane; the withers are prominent, the back long and straight, the croup wide and sloping, the tail well set-on, long and full, the chest deep, and the shoulder fairly long and sloping. The legs are sturdy, well-muscled and slender, with broad, clean joints, clearly defined tendons, and a well-formed foot, with tough horn.
History This pony lives in the New Forest, an area of woodland in southern England, which after 1079 was used by William the Conqueror as his hunting reserve. The present-day breed only developed in the nineteenth century when, at the request of Queen Victoria, Arab stallions were introduced into this area, subsequently followed by various other pony breeds, such as Welsh, Dartmoor, Exmoor, and Highland. The mares are crossed with horses of normal size to produce animals suited to light draft work, polo, and other equestrian sports.

137 FELL

Breed Fell.
Place of origin Great Britain (Cumbria).
Aptitudes Light draft and riding pony.
Qualities Strong, frugal, untiring.
Temperament Quiet but lively.
Conformation A pony of the mesomorphic type, with good conformation, standing 13–14 hands (1·32–1·42 m) at the withers; the coat is generally bay, brown, black or gray; coats devoid of white markings are preferred, though a small star and limited white markings to the legs are tolerated. The head is small, with a straight profile, small, pricked ears, lively, prominent eyes, and flared nostrils. The neck is well-proportioned, muscular and well set-on; the withers are quite pronounced, the back long and straight, the loins broad and strong, the croup short and sloping, the tail long and full, the chest broad and deep, and the shoulder long and sloping. The legs are sturdy and well-muscled, the cannons of considerable circumference, the pasterns not too long, the fetlocks feathered, and the hoof bluish and rounded.
History The name derives from the fells, the hilly moorlands on the western slopes of the Pennines, where the pony originated. It is descended from *Equus celticus* and perhaps from Frisian horses brought over by Roman legionaries. For centuries it was used down the Pennine lead mines as well as for transporting lead from the mines to the ports, and farm work. Today it is used as a riding pony, especially for trekking, and in harness it is popular for competitive driving. The Fell Pony Society was instituted in 1900, and the National Pony Society devotes a section to the breed in the Stud Book.

138 DALES

Breed Dales.
Place of origin Great Britain.
Aptitudes Pack and riding pony, farm work.
Qualities Strong and hardy.
Temperament Quiet and sensitive.
Conformation A pony of the mesomorphic type, with a maximum permitted height at the withers of 14·1 hands (1·44 m). The coat is usually black, bay, brown, or gray; white markings are rare. The head is small, with a straight profile, broad forehead, full forelock, small ears and eyes, and flared nostrils. The neck is not too long but muscular, with a full mane; the withers are quite prominent, the back not very long and sometimes hollow, the loins broad and muscular, the croup wide and sloping, the tail long and full, set-on rather low, the chest deep, and the shoulder quite straight. The legs are long, well-muscled and feathered at the extremities, and the hoof is bluish in color and tough.
History The name is taken from the dales, the valleys on the eastern side of the Pennines, where the breed originates. This breed, like the Fell, descends from the Celtic pony, but is of a heavier build, probably as a result of the influence of Welsh Cob blood, introduced in the nineteenth century. In the past it was used in the mines, for transport and for farm work. Today, with the advent of mechanization, it is finding a new rôle in the type of riding for pleasure known as pony-trekking and, as a harness pony in competitive driving.

139 EXMOOR

Breed Exmoor.
Place of origin Great Britain (Devon and Somerset).
Aptitudes Riding pony and light draft.
Qualities Speed, sturdiness.
Temperament Quiet.
Conformation A pony of the mesomorphic type, with a pleasing appearance and sturdy build. The height at the withers varies from 11·1–12·1 hands (1·14–1·25 m) in the male, while the maximum height for the female is 12 hands (1·24 m). The most common colors are bay, brown and mouse dun, always with a mealy muzzle and underbelly, extending to between the thighs; white markings are not permitted. The head is well-proportioned, with a straight profile, broad forehead, small, pointed ears, expressive, prominent eyes (toad eye), and flared nostrils. The neck is well-proportioned and well-formed, with a full mane; the withers are prominent, the back long and slightly hollow, the loins broad, the croup slightly sloping, the tail well set-on and full, the chest deep, and the shoulder sloping and muscular. The legs are sturdy and well-muscled, with long forearms and short cannons, and a small, tough hoof.
History This is probably the oldest pony breed in Great Britain. It possibly descends from the prehistoric wild horse used by the Celts, or it may have arrived in Cornwall at a time when Great Britain was still connected to Europe. The characteristic mealy markings are a sure sign of its antiquity. The conditions in which it lives, on the wild moorlands of southwest England, with their harsh winters, have toughened its physique to an exceptional degree.

140 SHETLAND

Breed Shetland.
Place of origin Scotland (Orkney and Shetland Islands).
Geographical distribution Worldwide.
Aptitudes Riding pony and light draft.
Qualities Strong, hardy, steady.
Temperament Lively, not always docile.
Conformation A pony of the mesomorphic type, standing 9–10 hands (0·90–1·06 m) at the withers and weighing 330–400 lb (150–180 kg). The coat may be any color, but the most common are piebald, skewbald, chestnut, bay or black. The head is small, but with pronounced jaws, a straight or concave profile, broad forehead, small ears, large eyes, and flared nostrils. The neck is short and muscular, broad at the base, with a long, full mane; the withers are wide, not very prominent, the back short and often hollow, the loins broad and muscular, the croup short and rounded, the tail long and full, and set-on high, the chest deep, the abdomen rounded, and the shoulder long and sloping. The legs are short and strong, with broad joints, pasterns of medium length, and the hoof small, round and hard.
History The discovery of fossilized remains suggests that this breed dates back to the Bronze Age, although it is considered by some to descend from horses brought to the islands in a sailing ship belonging to the Spanish Armada. In the nineteenth century it was used in the mines; today it is a very popular children's pony (although not always trustworthy) and is also used for drawing light carts, and for light farm work. Different breeding conditions in the United States have resulted in the development of a modified version of the breed.

141 HACKNEY PONY

Breed Hackney pony.
Place of origin Great Britain.
Aptitudes Light draft.
Qualities Fast.
Temperament Fiery, energetic.
Conformation A pony of the mesomorphic type, exactly resembling the Hackney, but smaller. The height at the withers is 12·1–14·1 hands (1·24–1·44 m). The coat may be bay, brown, black, gray, or roan; white markings are permitted. The head is light and elongated, with a straight or slightly convex profile, small pointed ears, and lively eyes. The neck is arched, muscular and well set-on; the withers are fairly pronounced, the back short and straight, the croup long and rounded, the tail, which is often cropped, is set-on high, the chest is wide and deep, and the shoulder nicely sloping and muscular. The legs are slender but strong, with broad, clean joints, long cannons, clearly defined tendons, and a well-formed foot, with tough horn. When the animal is at rest the hind legs are carried somewhat to the rear (straight hocked).
History This breed dates back to the early nineteenth century, although it did not become finally established until 1880. In addition to the Hackney horse, the Fell and the Welsh pony contributed to its formation and influenced its size. The objective in creating the breed was to produce a pony suitable for light draft, and it is used extensively in special showing classes for this breed. It does not have its own Stud Book, and is still registered in the Hackney's book.

142 WELSH MOUNTAIN PONY

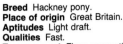

Breed Welsh Mountain pony.
Place of origin Wales.
Aptitudes Riding pony and light draft.
Qualities Hardy, sure-footed, and elegant in action.
Temperament Lively and intelligent.
Conformation A pony of the mesomorphic type, occupying Section A of the Welsh Stud Book, which only admits animals whose height at the withers does not exceed 12 hands (1·22 m). The coat may be any color except piebald and skewbald; gray, brown, and chestnut are the most common. The head is handsome, well-proportioned and well set-on, with a straight or slightly dished profile, a broad forehead, small, pricked ears, large, expressive eyes, and flared, prominent nostrils. The neck is well-formed and well set-on, quite arched, with a flowing mane; the withers are pronounced, the back short, the croup slightly sloping, the tail set-on high and elegantly carried, the chest deep, and the shoulder long, sloping and well-muscled. The legs are sturdy with good muscle formation, broad, solid joints, a long forearm, and a small, rounded foot, with tough horn.
History In appearance the Welsh Mountain pony is reminiscent of the Arab, but on a smaller scale, indicating a certain Oriental influence in its development. It seems that Julius Caesar himself encouraged the crossing of local ponies with stallions imported from the Orient, at a stud he had founded at Lake Bala. Distinguished in bearing, with a flowing, brilliant action, it is an ideal riding pony for young riders, and also performs elegantly in harness.

143 WELSH PONY

Breed Welsh Pony.
Place of origin Wales.
Geographical distribution Worldwide.
Aptitudes Riding pony, light draft.
Qualities Hardy, fine action.
Temperament Quiet but energetic.
Conformation A pony of the mesomorphic type occupying Section B of the Welsh Stud Book, which only admits animals whose height at the withers is between 12·2 and 13·2 hands (1·23–1.34 m). All colors of coat are permitted, from bay to brown, black, gray, chestnut and roan, only piebald and skewbald are excluded. The breed characteristics are similar to those of the Welsh Mountain pony.
History The Welsh pony is derived from the Welsh Mountain pony, but has received a greater contribution from the Hackney. Toward the end of the nineteenth century a small English Thoroughbred named Merlin was introduced into the breeding area, and seems to have been influential in the formation of the Welsh pony; for this reason animals registered in Section B of the Stud Book are also known as "Merlins." The Welsh pony has a flowing and energetic action, both at the trot and at the gallop.

---

144 WELSH PONY OF COB TYPE

Breed Welsh pony of Cob type.
Place of origin Wales.
Aptitudes Light draft, riding pony.
Qualitites Willing, hardy.
Temperament Energetic, lively.
Conformation A pony of the mesomorphic type displaying the characteristic "Cob" conformation, with shorter legs and a sturdier build; the maximum height at the withers is 13·2 hands (1·34 m). This pony is registered in Section C of the Welsh Stud Book. The head is of the pony type, with a straight profile; a coarse head with a convex profile (Roman nose) is considered objectionable. The ears are well set-on, and the eyes widely spaced and prominent, with a lively expression. The neck is long and well-carried, moderately slender in the female; the withers are slightly pronounced, the back short, with a slight depression toward the croup, the back and loins strong and muscular, the croup rounded, the tail well set-on, the chest wide and deep, the abdomen tucked up, and the shoulder strong, long and sloping. The legs are short, with some feather at the heels, a long forearm, nicely sloping pasterns, and a well-formed foot, with tough horn.
History This pony is also derived from the Welsh Mountain, but has had infusions of Hackney blood. Its stronger physical build enables it to carry heavier riders, even over rough and demanding terrains. It is, however, principally suited to light draft. In both uses this pony shows an energetic and lively action, which may well owe much to the Hackney influence.

145 HIGHLAND

Breed Highland.
Place of origin Scotland.
Aptitudes Riding and pack pony, light draft, farm work.
Qualitites Strong, hardy, excellent mountain horse.
Temperament Docile, sensitive.
Conformation A well-built pony of the mesomorphic type, of which there used to be two varieties: the Western Isles type, standing 12·2–14·2 hands (1·24–1·44 m) at the withers, and the Mainland type (Garron), with a maximum limit of 14·2 hands (1·44 m). This century there has been so much interbreeding between these types that a distinction is no longer made. The coat may be gray, palomino, mouse dun, bay, brown, black or liver chestnut (the latter with a silver mane and tail). The head is well-proportioned, with a straight or slightly convex profile, small ears, and expressive eyes. The neck is quite long, muscular and broad at the base, with a full mane; the withers are fairly prominent, the back is short and straight, the loins strong, the croup muscular, wide and slightly sloping, the tail long and full, the chest wide and deep, and the shoulder sloping and well-muscled. The legs are hard and well-muscled, with feather on the lower parts, broad, clean joints, short cannons, pasterns not too short, and a well-proportioned foot, with tough horn.
History The origins of this breed trace back to the Ice Age, as is testified by the presence of primitive features, such as zebra markings on the legs and the eel stripe, but its appearance also reveals infusions of Arab blood. A strong and sturdy animal, it is traditionally used in mountainous areas for deer hunting.

146 RIDING PONY

N.B. The Riding pony is generally considered a **type** rather than a breed.
Place of origin Great Britain.
Aptitude Riding pony.
Qualities Good jumper.
Temperament Quiet but energetic.
Conformation A pony of the dolichomorphic type, of excellent conformation, grouped into three different height categories; up to 12·2 hands (1·24 m), 12·3 to 13·2 hands (1·25–1·34 m), and 13·3 to 14·2 hands (1·35–1.44 m). All coat colors are permitted, as are white markings to the head and legs. The head is light, with a straight profile, small ears, and large, well-spaced eyes. The neck is long and well-formed; the withers are well-defined and high, the back straight and of medium length, the croup well-muscled and rounded, the tail well set-on, the chest broad and deep, and the shoulder nicely sloping. The legs are hard and clean, with broad joints, short cannons, and nicely proportioned feet, with tough horn.
History This breed is of recent creation, and was obtained by crossing English Thoroughbred and Arab stallions with native pony mares, including the Welsh, the Dartmoor and the Exmoor. The more robust Working hunter pony derives from the Riding pony, which it resembles in all but a few points of conformation, which have improved its performance.

147 CONNEMARA

Breed Connemara.
Place of origin Ireland (Connaught).
Aptitudes Riding pony, farm work.
Qualities Strong, hardy, good jumper.
Temperament Docile.
Conformation A pony of the mesomorphic type, standing 13–14·2 hands (1·32–1·44 m) at the withers; the coat may be gray, bay, brown, black or dun (often with eel stripe): roan and chestnut may occur. The head is small, with a straight profile small, ears, large eyes, and flared nostrils. The neck is long and well-formed, with a full mane; the withers are quite pronounced, the back long and straight, the croup well-muscled and slightly sloping, the tail full and long, the chest wide and deep, and the shoulder long and sloping. The legs are sturdy and well-muscled, with clean joints, long cannons, clearly defined tendons and a well-formed foot. The natural stance is correct.
History The breed's origins are not dissimilar to those of the Highland pony, both breeds having benefited from infusions of Arab blood; the Connemara, however, has also been influenced by contributions from the Spanish Horse and, more recently, from the English Thoroughbred and possibly the Fjord. It is reared in Ireland in the wild, but if transferred to more luxuriant pasture it shows a tendency to increase in stature and undergo certain structural modifications that set it apart from the original type. The Stud Book was established in 1924. This pony was used in the past for farm work, but today it is essentially a riding pony suitable for pony trekking and competitions. When crossed with horses of normal size it produces outstanding jumpers.

---

148 CAMARGUE

Breed Camargue.
Place of Origin France (Camargue).
Aptitudes Riding and pack pony.
Qualities Hardy, with good endurance.
Temperament Quiet.
Conformation A pony of the mesomorphic type, standing 13·1–14·2 hands (1·33–1·44 m) at the withers and weighing 660–880 lb (300–400 kg). The characteristic coat is gray, but bay and brown occur very rarely. the head is rather large, with pronounced jaws, a straight or convex profile, broad forehead, short, broad ears, and large, expressive eyes. The neck is quite short and muscular, broad at the base, with a full but shaggy mane; the withers are fairly pronounced, the back straight, the loins quite long, the flanks well-developed, the croup sloping, the tail full and flowing, the chest wide, and the shoulder straight and quite short. The legs are sturdy, with clean joints, a long forearm, and foot with tough horn.
History It is thought that this horse possibly descends from the prehistoric horse of Solutré. Once admired by Julius Caesar, it has more recently benefited from infusions of Arab and Barb blood. In the nineteenth century it was crossed with Arabs. English Thoroughbreds, Anglo-Arabs, and Postier-Bretons, but this did not result in modifications to the type. This pony lives in the wild in the Camargue region of southern France in the Rhône delta. Used by the *gardiens*, the herdsmen of the famous black bulls of the region, this pony risked extinction toward the middle of the twentieth century. The breed has had its own register since 1967.

149 LANDAIS

Breed Landais (Barthais).
Place of origin France (Landes).
Aptitudes Riding pony, light draft.
Qualities Hardy, resistant to harsh weather conditions, undemanding.
Temperament Intelligent, but somewhat independent.
Conformation A pony of the mesomorphic type, standing 11·1–13 hands (1·15–1·33 m) at the withers; the coat may be bay, brown, black or chestnut. The head is small, with a straight profile, broad forehead, small, pricked ears, and large well-spaced eyes. The neck is quite long, broad at the base with a full mane; the withers are pronounced, the back short, wide and straight, the croup short and sloping, the chest not very well-developed, the abdomen rounded, and the shoulder nicely sloping. The legs are sturdy and robust, and the hoof hard.
History The breed originates in the region of the Landes, around Barthais de l'Adour, in southwest France. The breed now includes the Barthais, once considered as a separate breed, which is heavier and slightly taller. If it is true that this pony derives from horses depicted in the prehistoric cave paintings at Lascaux, then its origins must be remote. It is thought that the breed received contributions of Arab blood at the time of the Battle of Poitiers in as early as 732 AD, and, again, more certainly between 1900 and 1913. At the start of the twentieth century there were still around two thousand breed members, but it is now increasingly difficult to find purebreds because in 1946 the Landais was crossed with other breeds with the aim of achieving a heavier build. Now, by the use of Arab and Welsh stallions, efforts are being made to obtain the original type.

150 MÉRENS

Breed Mérens (Ariègeois)
Place of origin France (Ariège).
Aptitudes Farm work, riding, pack pony.
Qualities Hardy and strong, suited to mountainous regions.
Temperament Energetic.
Conformation A pony of the mesomorphic type, standing 13–14·1 hands (1·33–1·45 m) at the withers and weighing 770–1,100 lb (350–500 kg). The characteristic coat is black. The head is distinguished and expressive, not heavy, with a straight profile, a broad forehead, with thick forelock, small ears, and lively eyes. The neck is quite short, broad at the base, well-carried and with a full mane; the withers are not very pronounced, the back long, strong and straight, the croup well-muscled and sloping, the tail long and full, the chest wide, the girth deep, the abdomen quite tucked up, and the shoulder straight. The legs are short, but well-proportioned, with good joints, clearly defined tendons, and sound feet with tough horn. Cow hocks are frequent.
History The origins of this breed are thought to be fairly remote, and have been almost certainly influenced by Oriental blood. Selection began after 1908. In the past it was used in the Ariège department of southwest France as a beast of burden for hauling timber and minerals. Following the advent of motorization it is now used for other purposes, such as pony trekking in mountainous areas. In appearance this pony resembles the Dales pony. The Stud Book for the breed was instituted in 1948, and is kept by the Syndicat d'Élevage du Cheval de Mérens.

151 FRENCH SADDLE PONY

Breed French Saddle Pony (Selle Français).
Place of origin France.
Aptitudes Riding pony.
Qualities Good jumper.
Temperament Quiet but energetic.
Conformation A pony of the dolichomorphic type, standing 12·1–14·2 hands (1·24–1·44 m) at the withers. All colors are permitted. The head is small, with a straight or slightly convex profile, average-sized ears, and lively eyes. The neck is long and well-formed, the withers prominent, the back straight, the croup sloping, the tail well set-on, the chest wide and deep, the abdomen tucked up, and the shoulder long and sloping. The legs are strong with large, clean joints, clearly defined, and a well-proportioned foot, with tough horn.
History This very recent breed was created for the same purposes as the English Riding pony. Its development has involved crossing selected mares belonging to breeds of native ponies with Arab, Connemara, New Forest and Welsh stallions. Its section of the French Pony Stud Book also includes animals produced by crossing Arab stallions with Connemara, New Forest and Welsh pony mares, and Selle Français, Connemara and New Forest stallions with Mérens, Basque and Landais mares. As well as competing in competition events, jumping and dressage it proves a first-rate harness pony.

152 GALICIAN AND ASTURIAN PONY

Breed Galician and Asturian (Asturçon).
Place of origin Spain (Galicia and Asturia).
Aptitudes Riding pony, light draft.
Qualities Hardy, frugal.
Temperament Docile, tractable.
Conformation A pony of the meso-dolichomorphic type, standing 11·2–12·3 hands (1·15–1·30 m) at the withers. The most common coats are brown and black with no white markings, although a small white star on the forehead is admitted. Although the head is not large it is rather heavy, with a straight profile, small ears, and large, lively eyes. The neck is quite long and thin with a flowing mane; the withers are not too high, the back straight, the croup sloping, the tail set-on low, the chest deep, the abdomen rounded, and the shoulder straight. The legs are tough with broad joints, short cannons, and a well-proportioned foot with tough horn.
History This pony's origins are closely related to those of the Celtic pony. Today it lives high in the Asturian mountains such as the Sierra de Sueve, but the most important group is concentrated in the western part of Asturia. With the difficult living conditions and lack of human intervention the breed has run the risk of becoming extinct. This danger has been averted thanks to its hardiness and ability to find food in areas inaccessible to larger horses. In winter the coat becomes longer, thicker and lighter in color, giving it a wild appearance. Recently, the importance of this pony has been realized and associations have been formed to protect it.

153 BASQUE

Breed Basque pony (Pottok).
Place of origin Spain (Basque Provinces and Navarra), France (southwest).
Aptitudes Riding pony, farm work, light draft.
Qualities Hardy, strong, sturdy, prolific, good jumper.
Temperament Quiet but energetic.
Conformation A pony of the mesomorphic type, standing 12–13 hands (1·20–1.32 m) at the withers; the characteristic coat is brown or black, but bay, chestnut, piebald and skewbald may also occur. The head is well-proportioned, with a straight or slightly convex profile, quite long ears, large, expressive eyes, flared nostrils, and an overhanging upper lip covered with whiskers. The neck is short and ewe-like, well set-on with a full but shaggy mane; the withers are high, the back long and straight, the croup rounded, the tail long and full, the chest wide, with rounded ribs, and the shoulder straight. The legs are clean and strong, with small, strong hooves. The hind legs may be cow-hocked.
History The Basque pony is said to descend from the prehistoric horse of the Solutré and may have been used by the Visigoths. It has received contributions of Arab blood and probably played a part in the formation of the Tarbais breed. The Basque, also known as the Pottok (meaning "small horse" in the Basque language), is considered an integral part of the Basque cultural heritage. It lives in the open in inhospitable surroundings. As a result of having to feed on spiny plants in the winter months, it develops a set of whiskers on its upper lip as protection. These disappear as soon as the weather is warmer and it is able to change its diet. It proves a good riding pony and is used for mountain trekking holidays.

154 SORRAIA

Breed Sorraia.
Place of origin Portugal.
Geographical diffusion Spain and Portugal.
Aptitudes Riding and pack pony.
Qualities Good endurance, frugal.
Temperament Independent but tractable.
Conformation A pony of the meso-dolichomorphic type, standing 12·2–13 hands (1·24–1·32 m) at the withers; the coat may be dun, gray or palomino, with zebra markings on the legs, and an eel stripe. The head is quite large, with a straight or slightly convex profile, and long ears, with black tips. The neck is long and slender, but not attractively shaped; the withers are quite high, the back straight, the croup slightly sloping, the tail set-on low, the chest not well-developed, and the shoulder not very muscular but quite straight. The legs are long and solidly built, with long pasterns, and a well-proportioned foot.
History This breed comes from the western region of the Iberian peninsula in the area north of Lisbon, crossed by the river Sorraia and its tributaries. Changes in the ecological balance of its natural habitat have had adverse effects on the breed causing a drastic reduction in the number of ponies still in existence. Its origins are thought to be remote as it shows a resemblance to the Asiatic wild horse and to the Tarpan.

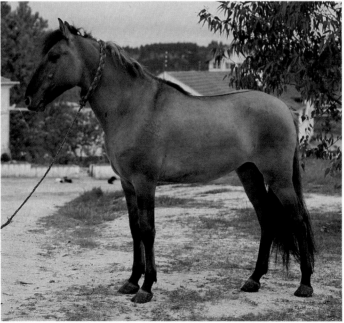

155 GARRANO

Breed Garrano (Minho).
Place of origin Portugal (Minho and Tras os Montes).
Aptitudes Riding and pack pony, farm work.
Qualities Strong, hardy.
Temperament Docile, quiet.
Conformation A pony of the mesomorphic type, standing 10–12 hands (1·02–1·22 m) at the withers; the coat is generally chestnut. The head is not large, but rather heavy, with a straight profile, small ears, and large, lively eyes. The neck is fairly long; the withers are not very pronounced, the back not always straight, the croup sloping, the tail set-on low, the chest deep, the abdomen rounded, and the shoulder straight. The legs are robust and solid, with broad joints, short cannons, and well-proportioned feet, with tough horn.
History This pony originated in the Portuguese regions of Minho and Tras os Montes, which lie along the banks of the River Minho on the border with Spain. It is a very old breed and resembles horses depicted in cave-paintings dating back to the Paleolithic era, proving that it has remained virtually unaltered in appearance for thousands of years. In more recent history it has received repeated infusions of Arab blood, although none of these appears to have left its mark. In the sixteenth century it gave rise, in South America, to the Galiceño, and even earlier than that it probably participated in the formation of the Andalusian. Until quite recently it was used in its region of origin for traditional trotting races.

---

156 BARDIGIANO

Breed Bardigiano (Bardi horse).
Place of origin Italy (Bardi).
Aptitudes Riding pony, farm work, medium-heavy draft.
Qualities Robust, hardy.
Temperament Quiet, docile, but quite highly strung.
Conformation A pony of the mesomorphic type, standing 13·1–14·1 hands (1·35–1·45 m) at the withers; males under 13·2 hands (1·37 m) are not admitted. The coat is bay, brown or black; chestnut and light bay are not admitted, and neither is bay with a blaze with too much lateral extension; limited white markings to the legs are permitted, as is a small star. The head is small, with a straight or concave profile, broad forehead, with an abundant forelock, small, pricked ears, and expressive eyes. The neck must be of a good length and broad at the base (preferably arched with a full mane); the withers are wide but not very pronounced, the back of medium length and straight, the loins short and broad, the croup wide and moderately sloping, the tail long, full and well set-on, the chest wide, deep and muscular, the girth deep, the abdomen clean and well-shaped, and the shoulder very muscular, of a good length and nicely sloping. The legs are not long, but have broad, clean joints, a fairly long forearm, muscular, rounded thighs, short cannons and pasterns, and a broad hoof, preferably with black, hard horn.
History This breed probably descends from the horse of Belgian Gaul that came to the Appenine region of Emilia in Italy during the barbarian invasions. In appearance and size it resembles the English Dales pony and the French Mérens. It is a useful mount for pony trekking.

157 AVELIGNESE

Breed Avelignese (Haflinger).

Place of origin Italy (Avelengo in Val Venosta).

Geographical distribution Italy (especially the Alto Adige), Austria, Switzerland, and Germany (in Austria and Bavaria it is bred under the name of Haflinger, the German for Avelignese).

Brand The registered firebrand takes the form of an eidelweiss with, in the center, HI for Italy or H for Austria.

Aptitudes Medium-heavy draft, farm work, riding or pack pony.

Qualities Resistant to fatigue and discomfort; hardy, frugal.

Temperament Docile, quiet, very trustworthy.

Conformation A pony of the mesomorphic type, the males standing 12·3–14 hands (1·30–1·42 m) at the withers, and the females 12·2–13·3 hands (1·28–1·40 m); the weight averages about 990 lb (450 kg). The coat is generally a magnificent chestnut, preferably golden, with forelock, mane and tail of a lighter shade; a blaze is common; white markings on the legs tend not to be extensive. The head is quite light, clean and expressive, with a slightly concave profile, a broad forehead, full forelock, lively eyes, small, mobile ears, thin lips, and the groove between the jaws open and well-defined. The neck, which is muscular, broad at the base and tapering, is well set-on, with an attractive mane; the withers are moderately pronounced, lean, and quite broad, the back is broad, short and generally straight (sometimes slightly hollow), the loins are short, rounded and fairly broad (preferably split), the croup is very muscular and moderately sloping, the tail, set-on low, is long and flowing, the chest full and muscular, high and wide, the girth deep, with well-sprung ribs, the abdomen well-formed and tucked up, and the shoulder nicely sloping, muscular and well set-on. The legs are short, with broad, hard joints, a strong forearm, muscular thighs, clean, straight hocks, short, clean cannons, short pasterns, and a well-formed foot, with a sound, hard hoof; the natural stance is correct.

History Little is known about the very early origins of this ancient breed, but its history can be traced back to the Middle Ages. It would seem to derive from a stallion sent from the Kingdom of Burgundy by Louis IV, King of Germany, as a gift to his son, the Margrave Louis of Brandenburg on the occasion of his marriage in 1342 to Princess Margaret Maultasch of the Tyrol: it is thought that this stallion gave rise to a small, sturdy horse, not unlike the present-day Avelignese. Another possibility is that it descends from horses abandoned in the valleys of the Tyrol by the Ostrogoths fleeing from Byzantine troops after the surrender of Conza (555 AD); this would explain the high percentage of Arab blood in the Avelignese. The first theory seems the more likely, particularly as there is historical evidence that at that time there existed to the south of the Alps a breed of light horse resembling the Oriental, suited to both draft and saddle; it is from that horse, with appropriate crossings, that the characteristics of the present breed would have been established. The Arab influence on the Avelignese was reinforced more recently by the introduction of further Oriental blood in the mid-nineteenth century. The true foundation sire of the breed was the stallion Folie, registration number 249, born in Val Venosta in 1874 out of a local mare and sired by the Arab stallion El Bedavi XXII, registration number 133. The shape of the head of the Avelignese clearly shows its Arab origins. The reliable nature of this pony makes it an ideal mount for children and beginners, and it also proves well-suited to pony trekking holidays over mountainous terrain.

158 SARDINIAN

Breed Sardinian.
Place of origin Italy (Sardinia).
Geographical distribution Italy (Sardinia).
Aptitudes Farm work, riding pony.
Qualities Hardy, resistant, agile.
Temperament Lively, highly strung, intractable, rebellious.
Conformation A pony of the mesomorphic type; the female stands 12·1–12·2 hands (1·25–1·27 m) at the withers, and the male at 12·2–13·0 hands (1·28–1·32 m). The weight varies from 375 to 485 lb (170–220 kg). the coat is most commonly bay, brown, black or liver chestnut. The head is square, with a heavy jaw, the profile straight or slightly convex, and the forehead covered by a full forelock. The neck is strong, with a full mane; the body is low-slung, with not very pronounced withers, a slightly hollow back, sloping croup, low-set tail, and fairly sloping shoulder. The legs are slender, the thighs not very muscular, the cannons long and thin, the pasterns long, and the foot small but sound. The natural stance is often marred by cow hocks.
History Although clearly an ancient breed, little is known of its earliest origins and the first reliable references to it date from 1845. This pony lives in the wild in Sardinia on a plateau 2,000 ft (600 m) above sea level, where conditions are poor and the vegetation thick but scrub-like, with sparse pastures flourishing briefly only in late spring.

159 BOSNIAN

Breed Bosnian.
Place of origin Yugoslavia (Bosnia-Herzegovina).
Geographical distribution Yugoslavia.
Aptitudes Riding and pack pony, farm work, light draft.
Qualities Steady, tenacious, hardy.
Temperament Docile.
Conformation A pony of the mesomorphic type, standing 12·1–14 hands (1·25–1·42 m) at the withers; the coat may be bay, brown, black, gray, chestnut or palomino. The head is heavy, with a straight profile, full forelock, and small ears. The neck is rather short and muscular, with a full mane; the withers are not very pronounced, the back is straight, the croup slightly sloping, the chest wide and deep, and the shoulder long and sloping. The legs are short but well-muscled, the joints broad and clean, the tendons strong, and the foot well-formed.
History The similarity in appearance between this pony and the Hucul, would suggest that it also derives from the Tarpan. Its rather refined features also indicate that it has benefited from the influence of Oriental blood. Stallions are controlled directly by the state, while mares are left to private ownership. The close involvement of the state in the breeding program reflects the importance of the breed in its native Yugoslavia, where it is still used for farm work.

160 PINDOS

Breed Pindos.
Place of origin Greece (Thessaly and Epirus).
Geographical distribution Greece (Thessaly and Epirus).
Aptitudes Light farm work, riding and pack pony, light draft.
Qualities Stamina.
Temperament Quiet.
Conformation A pony of the mesomorphic type, tending toward the meso-dolichomorphic, compact in build but at the same time pleasing in appearance, standing 12–13 hands (1·21–1·32 m) at the withers. The coat is usually bay, black or gray. The head is well-proportioned and well set-on, with a straight or slightly convex profile and a broad forehead. The neck is long and well set-on; the withers are not very pronounced, the back short and straight, the croup sloping, the chest wide, and the shoulder muscular and very straight. The legs are long, and the natural stance good.
History This ancient breed, which has without doubt benefited from infusions of Oriental blood during its development, is bred in the mountainous regions of Thessaly and Epirus. It is still used today in these areas for light farm work, and as a pack and riding pony. The mares of the breed are often coupled with donkeys to produce mules.

---

161 SKYROS

Breed Skyros.
Place of origin Greece (island of Skyros).
Aptitudes Riding and pack pony, light farm work.
Qualities Trustworthy.
Temperament Quiet.
Conformation A pony of the mesomorphic type, not very attractive in appearance, standing 9·1–11 hands (0·94–1·12 m) at the withers. The coat may be gray, bay, brown, or palomino. The head is small but not well set-on, with a straight profile, broad forehead, and small ears and eyes. The neck is short and thick, and also not well set-on; the withers are not very pronounced, the back short and straight, the croup poorly developed and sloping, the tail low-set, the chest not well-developed, and the shoulder poorly conformed and straight. The legs are slender, and the natural stance often defective (cow hocks).
History This pony, a native of the Greek island of Skyros, bears some resemblance to the Tarpan, suggesting that it has very early origins. Although unattractive in appearance it is undoubtedly one of the few breeds still in existence to remain largely uncontaminated by foreign blood. On the island they are used principally as pack animals. Ponies taken away from the island can, if properly reared and fed, improve in appearance and be trained to become good riding ponies for children.

162 PENEIA

Breed Peneia.
Place of origin Greece (province of Peneia in the Peloponnese).
Geographical distribution Greece.
Aptitudes Pack and riding pony, light draft, light farm work.
Qualities Willing, frugal, hardy.
Temperament Quiet.
Conformation An attractive-looking pony of the mesomorphic type, varying greatly in height from 10·1 to 14 hands (1·04–1·43 m) at the withers. The coat is usually bay, black, chestnut or gray, but other colors may be found. The head is well-proportioned, the profile tends to be convex, and the ears are small. The neck is well-proportioned and well set-on; the withers are not very pronounced, the back is short and straight, the croup sloping, the tail set-on quite low, the chest wide and fairly deep, and the shoulder muscular and nicely sloping. The legs are long and the feet small, with tough horn.
History The origins of the breed are unclear, but the rather refined appearance of this pony reveals a certain Arab influence. In its country of origin it is used mainly as a pack animal; it is willing and tireless, and for this reason the stallions are used in the production of hinnies (halfbreds).

163 VIATKA

Breed Viatka
Place of origin Soviet Union (Baltic States.
Aptitudes Farm work, light draft.
Qualities Fast, lively.
Temperament Quiet, but energetic and willing.
Conformation A pony of the mesomorphic type, standing 13–14 hands (1·32–1·42 m) at the withers; the coat is usually bay, gray, roan, mouse dun, palomino, or dun; in the last three an eel stripe and zebra markings on the legs may occur, with black mane and tail. The head, which is not large and has rather pronounced jaws, is not very well set-on and has a rather snub profile, a full forelock, medium-length ears, set well apart, bright and lively eyes, and flared nostrils. The neck is of medium length, but broad and muscular with a long, full mane; the withers are moderately pronounced, the back long and straight, the croup muscular and quite sloping, the tail set-on rather low, but full and flowing, the chest wide and deep, the abdomen tucked up, and the shoulder sloping and muscular. The legs are solid, well-muscled, with broad, clean joints, fairly short cannons, strong tendons, long pasterns, and a well-formed hoof.
History The breed descends from the old Klepper and the Konik. It is a sturdy animal, suitable for farm work and also for drawing troikas. Its action at the trot does not cover much ground, but this is an advantage on tiring, snow-covered terrain. The importance attributed to the breed today is such that it is rigorously controlled by the state.

164 KAZAKH

Breed Kazakh.
Place of origin Soviet Union (Kazakhstan).
Geographical distribution Soviet Union (Kazakhstan).
Aptitudes Riding pony.
Qualities Frugal, hardy, great stamina.
Temperament Willing, quiet.
Conformation A pony of the mesomorphic type, standing 12·1–13·1 hands (1·24–1·35 m) at the withers. It is bred as two distinct types: the Dzhabe and the Adaev. The Dzhabe, which has a coarse head and shortish neck, is generally bay or liver chestnut, although brown, bay and mouse dun are also found. The Adaev, has a light head, and a small, compact body with prominent withers and a straight back, and may be bay, gray, palomino or chestnut only.
History The similarity of this breed to the Asiatic wild horse is clear, although its appearance has been refined by considerable infusions of Don blood. Its hardiness is legendary, and the Kazakh is capable of finding food even in the most arid regions at the edges of the desert, or from snow-covered land. The Dzhabe is very resistant to both cold and fatigue, unlike the Adaev type, which has been more refined by infusions of Akhal-Teké, Iomud and Karabair blood and is thus less well-suited to harsh conditions.

165 ZEMAITUKA

Breed Zemaituka (Zhmud)
Place of origin Soviet Union (Lithuania).
Aptitudes Farm work, light draft.
Qualities Frugal, very resistant to fatigue.
Temperament Quiet, but energetic and willing.
Conformation A pony of the mesomorphic type, standing 13–13·1 hands (1·33–1·35 m) at the withers; the coat is usually bay, brown, black, mouse dun, dun or palomino; in the last three an eel stripe is common. The head is of medium size and rather coarse, not well set-on, with a straight profile, broad forehead, small ears, and expressive eyes. The neck is of medium length, broad and muscular; the withers are low and also of medium length, the back short and straight, the croup sloping, the tail set-on low, the chest deep, and the shoulder straight but well-muscled. The legs are short, but reasonably well-muscled, with poor joints, especially the hocks, sloping pasterns, of a good length, and a well-formed foot with tough horn.
History The frequent appearance of the ancestral coats with the characteristic eel stripe, reveals the ancient origins of this breed, which is thought to descend from the Asiatic wild horse. Although the breed may have benefited from infusions of Arab blood, it is not possible to detect this from its features. Clearly, living conditions have made it strong and exceptionally frugal, indifferent to cold and fatigue, but this at the exense of aesthetic qualities, in which respect it has shown itself resistant to all improving influences. This pony is capable of covering 40 miles (60 km) in a single day.

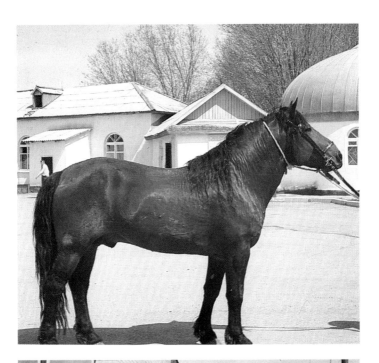

166 BASHKIR

Breed Bashkir (Bashkirsky).
Place of origin Soviet Union.
Geographical distribution Soviet Union.
Aptitudes Riding pony, light draft.
Qualities Strong, hardy.
Temperament Docile, quiet.
Conformation A pony of the mesomorphic type, standing 13·1–14 hands (1·34–1·42 m) at the withers; the coat is usually bay, chestnut or palomino. The head is rather heavy, with a straight profile, full forelock, and small, pricked ears. The neck is short and strong, with a long, attractive mane; the withers are quite low, the back elongated and sometimes slightly hollow, the croup slightly sloping, the tail set-on low but full and flowing, the chest wide and deep, and the shoulder correctly sloping. The legs are short and hard, and the foot small, with tough horn.
History This is a very old breed, with similar origins to other ponies from the Soviet Union. There are two distinct types, the mountain type and the steppes type, both suitable for riding and draft work. The mountain type is smaller and lighter and is better suited to riding; the steppes type is heavier, and is used for drawing troikas. The Bashkir is sometimes improved by crossing with riding breeds, such as the Don and the Budyonny, with draft breeds, such as the Ardennes, or with trotting breeds.

167 BASUTO

Breed Basuto.
Place of origin Lesotho (Basutoland).
Aptitudes Riding pony.
Qualities Hardy.
Temperament Reliable, hard-working, tolerant.
Conformation A pony of the mesomorphic type, standing 14–14·1 hands (1·43–1·45 m) at the withers; the coat is generally chestnut, bay, brown or gray. The head is of medium size, but with a rather heavy jaw, a straight profile, and smallish but expressive eyes. The neck is long and not very muscular; the withers are quite prominent, the back long and straight, the croup sloping, the tail set-on low, the chest deep, and the shoulder fairly straight. The legs are slender, but strong, with clean joints, and a hard hoof.
History This breed is descended from the Cape Horses, which arrived in Basutoland (now Lesotho) at the time of the Zulu invasions around 1822. The Cape Horse derives from the Barb and Arab horses imported by the Dutch East India Company in 1653. Before being introduced into Basutoland, this horse benefited from further contributions from the Arab and the English Thoroughbred. The Basuto dates back to 1830, but human neglect and harsh environmental conditions have resulted in a progressive degeneration in type, that has made it hardy and courageous. This pony was used in the Boer War and also, which seems surprising in view of its present-day appearance, for flat racing and polo. Its endurance is legendary, and enables it to cover 65 miles (100 km) in a day, with a weight of over 220 lb (100 kg) in the saddle.

168 PONY OF THE AMERICAS

Breed Pony of the Americas.
Place of origin United States.
Aptitudes Riding pony.
Qualities Versatile, fast, good jumper.
Temperament Quiet, docile.
Conformation A pony of the meso-dolichomorphic type, standing 11·1–13·1 hands (1·14–1·34 m) at the withers: the coats are the same as the Appaloosa: snowflake, leopard, frost, marble, spotted blanket, and white blanket. The head is nicely proportioned, with a slightly dished profile, medium-size, well-pricked ears, and large, prominent eyes. The neck is well-formed and slightly arched; the withers are prominent, the back short and straight, the back and loins broad and well-muscled, the croup long, muscular and rounded, tending to be flat, the tail well set-on, the chest wide and deep, and the shoulder nicely sloping. The legs are solid, well-formed and well-muscled, with strong tendons, nicely-sloping pasterns, a well-proportioned foot, broad and high at the heel, and a vertically-striped hoof.
History This breed is of recent formation, dating back only to 1956; its foundation sire was Black Hand, by a Shetland stallion and out of an Appaloosa mare, of which Black Hand was an exact reproduction in miniature. Conformation is halfway between a Quarter Horse and an Arab, with the characteristic coat of the Appaloosa. Because of its many qualities it is used for a wide variety of sporting activities, such as trotting races, show jumping, flat racing, long-distance rides and trekking; it is an ideal mount for children.

169 ASSATEAGUE AND CHINCOTEAGUE

Breed Assateague and Chincoteague.
Place of origin United States (Assateague and Chincoteague islands).
Geographical distribution United States.
Aptitudes Light draft, riding pony.
Qualities Resistant to harsh weather conditions.
Temperament Rebellious, stubborn.
Conformation Ponies of the mesomorphic type, standing about 12 hands (1·22 m) at the withers. All colors are found; piebald and skewbald coats are common. The head is long, with a straight profile, a longish neck, moderately pronounced withers, a straight back, slightly sloping croup, and a straight shoulder. The legs are solid.
History These ponies probably descend from a group of horses that survived a shipwreck at the beginning of the colonial period in America. The island of Assateague, off the coast of Virginia and Maryland, is uninhabited by man, enabling these animals to reproduce without restriction. The conformation of the animal, has gradually degenerated, giving it a somewhat deformed appearance. Every year, on the last Thursday and Friday in July, a group of ponies is swum across the channel to the island of Chincoteague to be auctioned. The shape of the heads of these animals gives them the appearance of small horses rather than of true ponies.

170 SABLE ISLAND PONY

Breed Sable Island pony.
Place of origin Canada (Sable Island).
Geographical distribution Canada (Sable Island).
Aptitudes Riding pony, light draft.
Qualities Strong, frugal.
Temperament Docile if domesticated young.
Conformation A pony of the mesomorphic type, standing about 14 hands (1·42 m) at the withers; the coat may be bay, brown, black, gray or chestnut. The head is heavy, with a straight profile, broad forehead, and rather large ears, with the tips turned inward. The neck is quite short, and broad at the base; the withers are quite prominent, the back short and straight, the croup sloping, the girth full, but not too deep, the abdomen bulky, and the shoulder quite straight. The legs are strong, with short cannons, and a small hoof.
History This pony's presence on this Atlantic island off the coast of Nova Scotia is owed to the importation from New England of a group of predominantly French animals at the start of the eighteenth century. The island has little natural vegetation, no trees, and a harsh climate, especially in winter. These inhospitable conditions have tempered the build of these ponies, which have become incredibly hardy. They live in small groups consisting of one stallion and 6–8 mares. Altogether there are about three hundred ponies on the island, very few of which merit attention.

171 GALICEÑO

Breed Galiceño.
Place of origin Mexico.
Geographical distribution Mexico, United States.
Aptitudes Riding and pack pony, light draft, farm work.
Qualities Speed and endurance, versatile, good jumper.
Temperament Docile, courageous, intelligent.
Conformation A pony of the mesomorphic type, standing 12–13·2 hands (1·21–1·37 m) at the withers, and weighing 620–750 lb (280–320 kg). The coat is usually bay, black or chestnut; piebald, skewbald and albino are not permitted. The head is of average size, with a straight profile, and lively, expressive eyes. The neck is quite short but muscular; the withers are quite pronounced, the back short, the croup sloping, the chest narrow but deep, and the shoulder quite straight. The legs are strong and long, but the natural stance is not always correct; the foot is small.
History Descended from the Garrano, this pony originated in the Spanish region of Galicia, and was taken across the ocean to Mexico in the sixteenth century by the Spanish *conquistadores*. In Mexico it is used for farm work and as a pack and draft pony. Since 1959 it has been exported to the United States, where it is used as a riding pony for children. It has proved to be a good jumper in events reserved for young competitors.

172 FALABELLA

Breed Falabella.
Place of origin Argentina.
Geographical distribution Argentina, United States, Canada, Great Britain.
Aptitudes Riding pony, light draft.
Qualities Very strong for its size.
Temperament Quiet, intelligent.
Conformation A pony of the mesomorphic type, very small in size, standing no more than 34 ins (86 cm) at the withers; the coat may vary, but the Appaloosa coat is much sought after. The head is small, with a straight or slightly dished profile, small ears, large eyes, and flared nostrils. The neck is well-formed, and the mane full; the withers are quite high, the back short and straight, the croup slightly sloping, the tail well set-on and flowing, the girth deep, and the shoulder sloping. The legs are rather slender, but well-built, with a well-formed foot.
History This is the smallest pony in the world and was bred by the Falabella family at their Recreo de Roca Ranch near Buenos Aires. It derives from the Shetland Pony and is the result of carefully selecting smaller animals. A limited contribution to the breed has been made by the English Thoroughbred. As well as a harmonious appearance it has a graceful action, earning it popularity, especially as a pet, in North America.

173 AUSTRALIAN PONY

Breed Australian pony.
Place of origin Australia.
Geographical distribution. Australia.
Aptitudes Riding pony.
Qualities Strong, healthy; well-suited for young children.
Temperament Well-balanced.
Conformation A pony of the mesomorphic type, standing 12–14 hands (1·21–1·42 m) at withers. The coat is generally gray, although any color is admitted with the exception of piebald and skewbald. The head is light, with a straight profile, well-proportioned, pointed ears, lively eyes, and a full forelock. The neck is well-formed and well set-on, arched, and with a very full mane; the withers are quite high, the back short and straight, the croup sloping, the chest well-developed, the girth full and deep, the shoulder long and nicely sloping. The legs are short with good bone and large joints, short cannons, clean strong tendons, long, nicely sloping pasterns, and a well-formed foot. The natural stance is good.
History This pony derives from a variety of breeds, including the Welsh Mountain pony, the Exmoor, the Shetland and the Timor, with some contribution from the English Thoroughbred and the Arab. Evidence of this last can be seen in some traits of the head. It is gifted with a flowing and attractive action, for which it is especially valued.

BREEDS NOT ILLUSTRATED

SYRIAN

Breed Syrian (Syrian Arab).
Place of origin Syria.
Geographical distribution Arab countries, Europe.
Aptitudes Riding horse.
Qualities Long-lived, fast, good endurance.
Temperament Energetic, lively.
Conformation A horse of the mesomorphic type, standing 14·2–15·2 hands (1·48–1·52 m) at the withers; the coat is gray or chestnut. Its elegant bearing resembles the Arab, from which it differs only in its larger size, the slightly wild expression of the eyes, and in its less harmonious, more angular conformation.
History This is the horse of the Bedouins, by whose side it has always existed, putting to the test its strength and endurance, tempered by all the hardships of desert life. Its origins are ancient and similar to those of the Arab, from which it is probably descended. Some believe it is an even better riding horse than the Arab, especially if reared by the Anazeh tribe.

BHUTIA

Breed Bhutia.
Place of origin India (Himalayas).
Aptitudes Riding horse.
Qualities Frugal, good endurance, well-suited to mountainous regions.
Temperament Not very reliable, often unpredictable.
Conformation A pony of the mesomorphic type, with clear Asiatic characteristics; standing 13–13·1 hands (1·32–1·34 m) at the withers. The coat is gray. The head is not large, but with pronounced jaws, a straight profile, a rather short neck, with a thick, shaggy mane; the withers are low, the back straight, the croup slightly sloping, the tail well set-on, the chest deep, and the shoulder quite straight. The legs are short and strong.
History This pony from the Himalayas, probably shares its origins with the native Tibetan and the Spiti, with which two breeds, given the geographical proximity, there has no doubt been close contact and interbreeding. Although the Bhutia is perhaps the least attractive of the three breeds from an aesthetical point of view, functionally it still proves useful as a pack pony in its natural environment, where the high mountainous slopes are inaccessible to other breeds not native to the region.

BURMESE

Breed Burmese (Shan).
Place of origin Burma.
Geographical distribution Burma.
Aptitudes Riding and pack pony.
Qualities Strong, with good endurance.
Temperament Active but not always reliable, often unpredictable.
Conformation A small and rather plain-looking pony of the mesomorphic type, standing about 13 hands (1·32 m) at the withers. The coat is usually bay, brown, black, gray or chestnut. The head is small and light, with a straight profile, and almond-shaped eyes. The neck is well-proportioned, and quite muscular; the withers are not very pronounced, the back straight and fairly long, the croup sloping, the girth deep, and the shoulder not very sloping. The legs are slender but strong, and the foot small with strong horn.
History This pony is bred by the hill tribes in Shan State in eastern Burma. It shows many similarities to the Manipuri, and although it is taller, slower, and not as quick off the mark, it was nevertheless used in the past as a polo pony by British colonials, who had to make do with this rather inferior breed in the

absence of anything better. Aesthetically it is not as elegant as the Manipuri, and is less compact, with a less sloping shoulder, suggesting that this breed has not been so influenced by the Arab. It is a very sure-footed and hardy animal, ideally suited to transporting goods and people in mountainous areas.

SUMBA AND SUMBAWA

Breed Sumba and Sumbawa.
Place of origin Indonesia (islands of Sumba and Sumbawa).
Geographical distribution Indonesia (Sumba and Sumbawa).
Aptitudes Riding and pack pony.
Qualities Good endurance.
Temperament Willing, docile.
Conformation A pony of the mesomorphic type, standing about 12 hands (1·22–1·22 m) at the withers. The coat is varied, the most common color being dun, with an eel stripe, and dark tail, mane, and points. The head is slightly on the heavy side, with a straight profile, and typically almond-shaped eyes. The neck is short and broad, with a shaggy mane; the withers are not very pronounced, the back quite long, the croup sloping, the girth quite deep, and the shoulder straight. The legs are short and strong, although fairly slender, and the foot is well-proportioned.
History These two ponies bear a close resemblance to the Chinese and Mongolian ponies, suggesting that they may have common origins. In Indonesia these breeds are used in "dancing" competitions, when they are ridden bareback by young boys, while a "dance master' directs the movements. The ponies have bells attached to their knees, which ring in time to the tom-toms.

NIGERIAN

Breed Nigerian.
Place of origin Nigeria.
Geographical distribution Nigeria.
Aptitudes Riding and pack pony, light draft.
Qualities Strong, enduring.
Temperament Willing, docile.
Conformation A pony of the mesomorphic type, compact in form, standing 14–14·1 hands (1·42–1·44 m) at the withers. The coat may be any color. The head is quite flat, with a straight profile, and small, pricked ears. The neck is rather short and not striking; the withers are quite pronounced, the back short and straight, the croup sloping, the girth quite deep, and the shoulder nicely sloping and well-shaped. The legs are strong, and of medium length, and the foot has strong horn.
History This breed probably descends from the Barb, which was brought to Nigeria by nomadic tribes; the markedly sloping croup seems proof of this theory. This pony has more the appearance of a horse, and is at the upper limit of the pony category. In appearance it is compact and pleasing, although the hindquarters are weak and poorly developed.

GREAT CHAMPIONS OF TODAY

It is important to study the genealogy of a race horse, since by analysing the characteristics of its ancestors it is possible to predict the particular aptitudes of a future champion. Similarly, for the same reason it is just as important when selecting animals for breeding to take into consideration the pedigree and carefully evaluate the blood strains that are represented. In fact, selective breeding, which aims to improve the characteristics of a breed by coupling high quality animals of the same breed, although based on the morphological and functional qualities of the breed, can not dismiss the genealogy.

When examining a pedigree if one progenitor should appear several times in the last six generations this is described as "inbreeding," while if this does not occur it is "outcrossing." Consequently, if for example in the ancestry of an English Thoroughbred, the name of Nearco appears twice in the third generation, twice in the fourth and three times in the fifth, this is called inbreeding of Nearco $3\times3\times4\times4\times5\times5\times5$, indicating by this formula the number of times and in which generations, the name of this famous stallion occurs. The most restricted form of inbreeding is obviously incest; in this case the formula 1×2 is given if a horse or mare is coupled with one of its parents, 1×3 if coupled with one of its grandparents, and 2×2 if mated with its half brother or sister, either on the paternal or maternal side, even though two horses are generally only considered to be half brothers or sisters if they are both out of the same mare. By inbreeding it should technically be possible to fix or enhance the qualities present in the genetic heritage of both the stallion and the mare, however, occasionally it occurs that the combination of the defects in both animals predominates, with unfavorable results for the progeny.

The idea of outcrossing is to create new genetic combinations by introducing new blood strains, with the hope of possibly creating a great champion possessing the qualities, either apparent or latent, of his forebears.

There have been many supporters of both inbreeding and outcrossing. In the first group is the famous French breeder Marcel Boussac, and in the second Federico Tesio, who has created many famous champions such as the outstanding Nearco and Ribot.

Nearco's influence on the present-day English Thoroughbred is exceptional and has been expressed principally through his descendants: Nasrullah (d.b. 1940) and Nearctic (d.b. 1954) although, as often occurs, out of all his offspring these two were certainly not the best performers on the racecourse. Of the two bloodlines the one that currently predominates is perhaps the second thanks to Northern Dancer (b. 1961 from Nearctic and Natalma) and to his progeny, which includes Nijinsky (b. 1967) winner of the English Triple Crown (2,000 Guineas, Derby and St. Leger) and The Minstrel (c. 1974) winner of the English as well as the Irish Derby.

Moving on to trotting breeds the trotters Star's Pride (d.b. 1947) and Speedster (b. 1954) have had a similar influence on the American breed (Standardbred), as have Fandango (b. 1947), and Kerjacques (c. 1954), sire of the phenomenal Une de Mai (f.c. 1964), on the French Trotter. Another French stallion to have very good results at stud is Carioca II (1946), from the American line that descends from Hambletonian 10, through Sam Williams, from whom Idéal du Gazeau (b. 1974), Lurabo (c. 1977) and Ourasi (c. 1980) descend.

Golden Fleece m.b. born in the United States in 1979
Owner: R. Sangster
Breeder: Mr. and Mrs. Paul Hexter
Racing career: 4 races run (2- and 3-year-olds) 4 wins
Most important wins: Derby Stakes
British 3-year-old champion in 1982
Died in 1984 from cancer of the stomach

Golden Fleece m.b. 1979	Nijinsky b. 1967	Northern Dancer b. 1961	**Nearco**
		Nearctic d.b. 1954	Lady Angela
		Natalma b. 1957	Native Dancer
			Almahmoud
		Flaming Page b. 1959	Bull Lea
		Bull Page b. 1947	Our Page
		Flaring Top c. 1947	Menow
			Flaming Top
	Exotic Treat c. 1971	Vaguely Noble b. 1965	Aureole
		Vienna c. 1957	Turkish Blood
		Noble Lassie b. 1956	**Nearco**
			Belle Sauvage
		Rare Treat c. 1952	Equestrian
		Stymie c. 1941	Stop Watch
		Rare Perfume b. 1947	Eight Thirty
			Fragrance

Sagace m.b. born in France in 1980
Owner: D. Wildenstein
Breeder: Dayton Ltd
Racing career: 13 races run (3-, 4- and 5-year-olds) 8 wins
Most important wins: Prix de l'Arc de Triomphe (1984), Prix Ganay (1985), Prix d'Ispahan (1985); in 1985 demoted from 1st to 2nd place in the Prix de l'Arc de Triomphe for causing injury. Horse of the year in France in 1985.

Sagace m.b. 1980	Luthier d.b. 1965	Klairon b. 1952	Clarion b. 1944
			Djebel
			Columba
		Kalmia b. 1931	Kantar
			Sweet Lavender
	Flûte Enchantée b. 1950	Cranach b. 1923	Coronach
			Reine Isaure
		Montagnana c. 1937	Brantôme
			Mauretania
	Seneca b. 1973	Chaparral b. 1966	Val de Loir b. 1959
			Vieux Manoir
			Vali
		Niccolina c. 1950	Niccolò dell'Arca
			Light Sentence
	Schonbrunn b. 1966	Pantheon b. 1958	Borealis
			Palazzo
		Scheherazade d.b. 1952	Ticino
			Schwarzblaurot

El Gran Señor m.b. born in the United States in 1981
Owner: R. Sangster
Breeder: E.P. Taylor
Racing career: 8 races run (2- and 3-year-old) 7 wins
Most important wins: William Hill Dewhurst Stakes, 2000 Guineas, Irish Derby

El Gran Senor m.b. 1981	Northern Dancer b. 1961	Nearctic d.b. 1954	Nearco d.b. 1935	Pharos
				Nogara
			Lady Angela c. 1944	Hyperion
				Sister Sarah
		Natalma b. 1957	Native Dancer gr. 1950	Polynesian
				Geisha
			Almahmoud c. 1947	Mahmoud
				Arbitrator
	Sex Appeal c. 1970	Buckpasser b. 1963	Tom Fool b. 1949	Menow
				Gaga
			Busanda bl. 1947	War Admiral
				Businesslike
		Best in Show b. 1965	Traffic Judge c. 1952	Alibhai
				Traffic Court
			Stolen Hour c. 1953	Mr. Busher
				Late Date

Spend A Buck m.b. born in the United States in 1982
Owner: Hunter Farm
Breeder: Rowe Harper - Irish Hill Farm
Racing career: 15 races run (2- and 3-year-olds) 10 wins
Most important wins: Kentucky Derby, Jersey Derby
Winner of a total of $4,220,689 during his career.

Spend A Buck m.b. 1982	Buckaroo b. 1975	Buckpasser b. 1963	Tom Fool b. 1949	Menow
				Gaga
			Busanda bl. 1947	War Admiral
				Businesslike
		Stepping High b. 1969	No Robbery b. 1960	Swaps
				Bimlette
			Bebop II b. 1957	Prince Bio
				Cappellina
	Belle de Jour b. 1973	Speak John d.b. 1958	Prince John c. 1953	Princequillo
				Not Afraid
			Nuit de Folies b. 1947	Tornado
				Folle Nuit
		Battle Dress b. 1966	Jaipur d.b. 1959	Nasrullah
				Rare Perfume
			Armorial b. 1955	Battlefield
				Tellaris

Shahrastani m.c. born in the United States in 1983
Owner: S.A. Aga Khan
Breeder: S.A. Aga Khan
Racing career: 6 races run (2- and 3-year-olds) 4 wins
Most important wins: Derby Stakes, Irish Derby

Shahrastani m.c. 1983	Nijinsky b. 1967	Northern Dancer b. 1961	Nearctic d.b. 1954	Nearco
				Lady Angela
			Natalma b. 1957	Native Dancer
				Almahmoud
		Flaming Page b. 1959	Bull Page b. 1947	Bull Lea
				Our Page
			Flaring Top c. 1947	Menow
				Flaming Top
	Shademah b. 1978	Thatch b. 1970	Forli c. 1963	Aristophanes
				Trensa
			Thong b. 1964	Nantallah
				Rough Shod
		Shamim c. 1968	Le Haar c. 1954	Vieux Manoir
				Mince Pie
			Diamond Drop c. 1963	Charlottesville
				Martine III

Lutin d'Isigny m.c. 1977 (France)
Owner: M.G. Corniere
Breeder: M.me J. Auvray
Racing career: still competing
Most important wins: Prix de Paris (Paris, 1984), Prix d'Amérique (Paris, 1985),
Roosevelt International Trot (New York, 1984), Challenge Cup (New York,
1984 and 1985) Trotter of the year in France in 1985

Lutin d'Isigny m.c. 1977 - 1'13''1/10 over the Km	Firstly b. 1971 - 1'15''	Querido II 1'17''	Fandango 1'20''	Loudéac 1'26''
				Tombelaine 1'30''
			Dladys	Hernani III 1'24''
				Gladys *
		Matinale 1'19''	Bourbonnais D	Ogaden 1'25''
				Narbonnaise D 1'28''
			Guitare d'Amour 1'37''	Petit Mamile 1'24''
				Valeur Or
	Dame d'Isigny b. 1969 - 1'20''	Queronville L 1'16''	Tigre Royal 1'22''	Esope 1'26''
				Hollyanne 1'23''
			Brescia	Jean Sans Peur 1'23''
				Genes 1'28''
		Voile au Vent II	Larré F 1'20''	Carioca II 1'26''
				Belle de Nuit F 1'25''
			Ol d'Aubigny	Goeland
				Etoile de Bony

*English Thoroughbred

Minou du Donjon m.c. 1978 (France)
Holder of the absolute record for horses born in France: 1'11"5 over the km, set in
Stockholm in 1985
Owner: J.L. Peupion
Breeder: Camille Bedier
Racing career: still competing
Most important wins: Prix de Belgique (Paris, 1985), Jubilee Cup (Stockholm, 1985),
Aby Stora Pris (Aby, 1985), Grand Prix Fernand Talpe (Kuurne, 1985), Copenhagen Cup
(Copenhagen, 1985)

			Quo Vadis 1916 - 1'25"
		Javari 1931 - 1'23"	Reluisante 1917 - 1'30"
	Vermont 1943 - 1'25"		Nembrod 1913 - 1'29"
		Action 1922 - 1'29"	Nouvelle 1913
Quioco c. 1960 - 1'15"			Sam Williams (USA) 1922 - 1'26"
		Lord Williams 1933 - 1'21"	Slim 1918 - 1'27"
	Beatrix 1945 - 1'26"		Fakir V 1927 - 1'28"
		Psappha 1937 - 1'35"	Fille de l'Air III 1927 - 1'30"
Minou du Donjon m.c. 1978 - 1'11"5/10 over the Km			Hernani III 1929 - 1'24"
		Quinio 1938 - 1'25"	Germaine 1928 - 1'29"
	Kerjacques 1954 - 1'19"		Loudeac 1933 - 1'26"
		Arlette III 1944 - 1'22"	Maggy II 1934 - 1'35"
Geribia c. 1972			Volontaire 1943 - 1'21"
		Jocrisse 1953 - 1'20"	Cartacalla 1946 - 1'32"
	Uribia 1964 - 1'21"		Au Vent 1944 - 1'25"
		Junia 1953 - 1'22"	Nevada IV 1935 - 1'26"

Meadow Road m.b. 1979 (Sweden)
Holder of the absolute world record for horses born in Europe and the world record for
horses of 4 years and above: 1'54''2/5 (1'11''1/10 over the km)
Owner: O. Rydstrand
Breeder: S. Palm
Racing career: 43 races run (2-, 3-, 4- and 5-year-olds) 34 wins
Most important wins: Gran Premio delle Nazioni (Milan, 1984), Elitlopp (Stockholm, 1985,
final), Statue of Liberty-Trot (Meadowlands, 1985, 1 mile/1,609 m), Statue of Liberty-Trot
(Meadowlands, 1985, 1½ miles/2,413 m)

Meadow Road m.b. 1979 - 1'11''1/10 over the Km	Madison Avenue (USA) b. 1971 - 1'13''5/10	Nevele Pride b. 1965 - 1'54''4/5 (TT)	Star's Pride d.b. 1947 - 1'57''1/5
			Worthy Boy bl. 1940 - 2'02''1/2
			Stardrift d.b. 1936 - 2'03''
		Thankful d.b. 1952 - 2'03''2/5 (TT)	Hoot Mon bl. 1944 - 2'00''
			Magnolia Hanover d.b. 1944 - 2'13''1/5
	Scenic Route b. 1966	Spectator 1958 - 1'59''4/5	Florican b. 1947 - 1'57''2/5
			Picturesque 1953
		Mimi Rodney b. 1962	Rodney b. 1944 - 1'57''2/5 (TT)
			Mimi Hanover b. 1945 - 2'09''
	Francessa (Sweden) b. 1972 - 1'21''	Frances Nib 1'17''3/10	Scotch Nibs 1'17''3/10
			Nibble Hanover b. 1936 - 1'58''3/4
			Hattie G 2'03''2/5
		Frances Bulwark 1'16''7/10	Bulwark 1'18''8/10
			Frances Great 2'08''1/2
	Petressa	Lord Peter 1'18''1/10	Peter Rutherford 1'21''6/10
			My Lady Hanover 1'25''5/10
		Comptesse 1'24''1/10	Ronald Day 2'07''1/4
			Mari Dennis 1'30''9/10

TT = Time Trial

Prakas m.b. 1982 (United States)
Holder of the absolute world record: 1'53''2/5 (1'10''5/10 over the km) taken from Du Quoin on August 31, 1985
Owner: H. Enggren, C. Vizzi, I. McKenzie
Breeder: Hans Enggren
Racing career: 29 races run (2- and 3-year-olds) 14 wins
Most important wins: Historic Cup, Beacon Course, Hambletonian Stake, World Trotting Derby, Beeders Crown
Trotter of the year in the United States in 1985

Prakas m.b. 1982 - 1'53''2/5				
	Speedy Crown b. 1968 - 1'57''1/5	Speedy Scot b. 1960 - 1'56''4/5	Speedster b. 1954 - 1'59''4/5	**Rodney** b. 1944 - 1'57''2/5 (TT)
				Mimi Hanover d.b. 1945 - 2'09''
			Scotch Love d.b. 1954 - 2'04''3/5 (TT)	Victory Song d.b. 1943 - 1'57''3/5
				Selka Scot b. 1945 - 2'13''3/5
		Missile Toe b. 1962 - 2'05''2/5	Florican b. 1947 - 1'57''2/5	Spud Hanover c. 1936 - 2'03''
				Florimel b. 1938 - 2'03''1/2
			Worth A Plenty b. 1954 - 2'02''2/5 (TT)	Darnley bl. 1940 - 1'59''3/4
				Sparkle Plenty b. 1948 - 2'07''3/5
	Prudy Hanover b. 1970 - 2'04''4/5	Star's Pride d.b. 1947 - 1'57''1/5	Worthy Boy bl. 1940 - 2'02''1/2	Volomite d.b. 1926 - 2'03''1/4
				Warwell Worthy b. 1932 - 2'03''3/4
			Stardrift d.b. 1936 - 2'03''	Mr. Mc Elwyn b. 1921 - 1'59''1/4 (TT)
				Dillcisco b. 1919 - 2'06''1/2
		Prudence N b. 1960 - 2'02''4/5	**Rodney** b. 1944 - 1'57''2/5 (TT)	Spencer Scott b. 1937 - 1'57''1/4 (TT)
				Earl's Princess Martha b. 1935 - 2'01''3/4 (TT)
			Prudence Hanover b. 1941 - 2'07''1/2	Calumet Chuck d.b. 1929 - 2'04''
				Grace Hanover b. 1929 - 2'05''

TT = Time Trial

Nihilator m.b. 1982 (United States)
Holder of the world record in pacing races: 1'49"3/5
Owner: Wall Street - Nihilator Syn
Breeder: Robert E. Gangloff
Racing career: 35 races run (2- and 3-year-olds) 33 wins
Most important wins: International Stallion (1984), Goshen Cup (1984), Potomac Pace (1984), Baltimoreas Series (final, 1984), Kentucky Sires (1984), Meadowlands Pace (1985), Little Brown Jug (1985), Dancer Memorial (1985), Jersey Cup (1985), Homecoming Pace (1985), Terrapin Pace (1985)

Nihilator m.b. 1982 - 1'49"3/5				
Niatross b. 1977 - 1'49"1/5 (TT)	Albatross b. 1968 - 1'54"3/5	**Meadow Skipper** d.b. 1960 - 1'55"1/5	Dale Frost bl. 1951 - 1'58"	**Hal Dale** - 2'02"1/4 / Galloway - 2'04"1/2
			Countess Vivian b. 1950 - 1'59"	King's Counsel - 1'58" / Filly Direct - 2'06"3/4
		Voodoo Hanover	Dancer Hanover b. 1957 - 1'56"4/5 (TT)	**Adios** - 1'57"1/2 (TT) / The Old Maid
			Vibrant Hanover	**Tar Heel** - 1'57" (TT) / Vivian Hanover
	Niagara Dream b. 1964 - 2'07"2/5	Bye Bye Byrd b. 1955 - 1'56"1/5 (TT)	Poplar Byrd b. 1944 - 1'59"3/5 (TT)	Volomite - 2'03"1/4 * / Ann Vonian - 2'01"1/4
			Evalina Hanover 1'59"2/5	**Billy Direct** - 1'55" (TT) / Adieu - 2'04"1/4 (TT)
		Scott b. 1946 - 2'05"2/5 *	Scamp	Guy Abbey - 2'06"3/4 * / Sweet Miss - 2'08"1/2 (TT) *
			Doris Spencer	Spencer - 1'59"3/4 (TT) * / Last Chance - 2'22"1/4 (TT) *
Margie's Melody b. 1976 - 1'55"4/5	Bret Hanover b. 1962 - 1'53"3/5	**Adios** b. 1940 - 1'57"1/2 (TT)	**Hal Dale** 1926 - 2'02"1/4	Abbedale - 2'01"1/4 / Margaret Hal - 2'19"
			Adioo Volo 1930 - 2'05"	Adioo Guy - 2'00"3/4 / Sigrid Volo - 2'04" (TT)
		Brenna Hanover b. 1956 - 2'01"	**Tar Heel** 1948 - 1'57" (TT)	**Billy Direct** - 1'55" (TT) / Leta Long - 2'03"3/4
			Beryl Hanover 1947 - 2'02"	Nibble Hanover - 1'58"3/4 * / Laura Hanover - 2'15"1/4 *
	Pretty Margie d.b. 1971 - 2'05"4	**Meadow Skipper** d.b. 1960 - 1'55"1/5	Dale Frost bl. 1951 - 1'58"	**Hal Dale** - 2'02"1/4 / Galloway - 2'04"1/2
			Countess Vivian b. 1950 - 1'59"	King's Counsel - 1'58" / Filly Direct - 2'06"3/4
		Margie's Storm d.b. 1962 - 2'06"	Storm Cloud gr. 1954 - 2'00"4/5 *	Scotland - 1'59"1/4 * / Queen Nib *
			My Margie d.b. 1955 - 2'06"2/5 *	Mighty Song - 2'00"2/5 (TT) ** / Margaret Castleton - 1'59"1/4 *

* Trotter   ** Pacer-trotter (2'02"3/5 TT)
TT = Time Trial

SELECT BIBLIOGRAPHY

Bongianni, M. *Great Horses*, London, 1984; *Champion Horses*, New York, 1984

Bongianni, M., and Mori, C. *Horses of the World*, London and New York, 1984

Churchill, P. *All Colour World of Horses*, London, 1978

Dossenbach, M. and H. *The Noble Horse*, Exeter, 1983

Edwards, E.H. (ed.), *A Standard Guide to Horse and Pony Breeds*, London, 1980

Edwards, E.H. (ed.), *Encyclopedia of the Horse*, London, 1977

Edwards, E.H., and Geddes, C. *The Complete Book of the Horse*, New York, 1974

Foster, C. *The Complete Book of the Horse*, London, 1983

Glyn, R. *The World's Finest Horses and Ponies*, London, 1971

Goodall, D.M. *Horses of the World – An illustrated survey of breeds of horses and ponies*, Newton Abbot, 1973

Goody, P.C. *Horse Anatomy*, London, 1976

Hope, C.E.G., and Jackson, G.N. *The Encyclopedia of the Horse*, London, 1973

Kays, J.M. *The Horse*, New York, 1969

Kidd, J., *et al. The Complete Horse Encyclopedia*, London, 1976

Phifer, K.G. *Track Talk*, New York, 1978

Reddick, K. *Horses*, Toronto and New York, 1976

Silver, C. *Guide to the Horses of the World*, Oxford, 1976

Whitlock, R. *Gentle Giants*, Guildford, 1976

INDEX

The number that appears next to each breed name refers to the corresponding entry. Where p. precedes the number this indicates the page.

Akhal-Teké 50
Albino 74
Altér-Real 8
American Cream 74
American Saddlebred 75
American Saddlehorse 75
Andalusian 5
Appaloosa 72
Arab 1
Arabian horse 1
Ardennais 92
Ariègeois 150
Asiatic wild horse 118
Assateague 169
Asturçon 152
Asturian pony 152
Australian pony 173
Australian Stock Horse 84
Auxois 91
Avelignese 157
Azteca 81

Bali 127
Barb 2
Bardigiano 156
Bardi horse 156
Barthais 149
Bashkir 166
Bashkirsky 166
Basque 153
Basuto 167
Batak 130
Belgian Ardennes 86
Belgian Barbant 86
Belgian Draft 86
Bhutia p. 240
Bosnian 159
Boulonnais 88
Breton 90
Brumby 85
Budyonny 52
Burmese p. 240

Calabrese 27
Camargue 148
Carpathian pony 116
Canadian Cutting Horse 80
Carthusian 6
Caspian 124
Cheval du Poitou 94
Chincoteague 169
Chinese 125
Cleveland Bay 13
Clydesdale 96
Comtois 89
Connemara 147
Criollo 83

Dales 138
Danubian 47

Dartmoor 135
Døle Gudbrandsdal 99
Don 51
Dutch Draft 103
Dutch Warm-blood 10

East Bulgarian 45
East Frisian 35
East Prussian 31
English Thoroughbred 12
Exmoor 139

Falabella 172
Fell 137
Finnish Universal 40
Fjord 131
Franches-Montagnes 107
Frederiksborg 18
Freiberger 107
French Anglo-Arab 20
French Ardennais 92
French Saddle Pony 151
French Trotter 19
Frisian 9
Furioso-North Star 44

Galiçeno 171
Galician pony 152
Garrano 155
German Cold-blood 105
Gelderland 11
Gidran Arabian 41
Gotland 134

Hackney 14
Hackney pony 141
Haflinger 157
Hanoverian 32
Highland 145
Hispano 4
Holstein 33
Hucul 116
Hungarian Anglo-Arabian 41

Icelandic pony 133
Iomud 53
Irish cob 17
Irish Draft 98
Irish Hunter 16
Italian Heavy Draft 108

Java 129
Jomud 53
Jutland 102

Kabardin 61
Karabair 60
Karabakh 62
Karacabey 67
Kathiawari 122

Kazakh 164
Kentucky Saddlebred 75
Kladruber 38
Konik 117
Kustanair 66

Landais 149
Latvian 65
Latvian Harness Horse 65
Lipizzaner 37
Lithuanian Heavy Draft 114
Lokai 63
Lusitano 7

Malapolski 48
Manipuri 120
Maremmana 23
Marwari 122
Mecklenburg 36
Merens 150
Metis Trotter 55
Minho 155
Missouri Fox Trotting Horse 76
Mongolian 119
Mongolian wild horse 118
Morgan 68
Murakoz 110
Murgese 24
Mustang 78

Nanfan 123
New Forest 136
New Kirghiz 57
Nigerian p. 241
Nonius 43
Noriker 106
Northlands 132
North Hestur 100
North Swedish Horse 100
North Swedish Trotter 100
Novokirghiz 57

Oberlander 106
Oldenburg 30
Orlov 56

Palomino 73
Paso Fino 82
Peneia 162
Percheron 87
Persano 26
Persian Arab 3
Pindos 160
Pinto 71
Pinzgauer 106
Pleven 46
Poitevin 94
Polish Anglo-Arab 48
Pony of the Americas 168

Pottok 153

Quarter Horse 69

Rhenish 105
Rhineland Heavy Draft 105
Riding pony
Russian Heavy Draft 112
Russian Trotter 55

Sable Island pony 170
Salerno 26
Sandalwood 128
San Fratello 29
Sardinian 158
Sardinian Anglo-Arab 25
Schleswig Heavy Draft 104
Selle Français 21
Shagya Arabian 42
Shan p. 240
Shetland 140
Shire 97
Sicilian 28
Skogsruss 134
Skyros 161
Sokolsky 109

Sorraia 154
South German Cold-blood
   106
Soviet Heavy Draft 111
Spanish Anglo-Arab 4
Spanish Mustang 78
Spiti 121
Standardbred 70
Suffolk Punch 95
Sumba p. 241
Sumbawa p. 241
Swedish Ardennes 101
Swedish Halfbred 39
Swedish Warm-blood 39
Swiss Warm-blood 22
Syrian p. 240

Tarpan 115
Tennessee Walking Horse
   77
Terek 59
Tersk 59
Tersky 59
Tibetan 123
Timor 126
Toric 64

Trait du Nord 93
Trait Percheron 87
Trakehner 31
Turkmen 54
Turkmene 54
Turkoman 54

Ukrainian Riding Horse 58

Viatka 163
Vladimir Heavy Draft 113

Waler 84
Welsh Cob 15
Welsh Mountain pony 142
Welsh pony 143
Welsh pony of Cob type 144
Westlands Pony 131
Weilkopolski 49
Wild Horse of Wyoming 79
Württemberg 34

Yomud 53

Zemaituka 165
Zhmud 165

PICTURE SOURCES

The abbreviations a, b, refer to the position of the photograph on the page (above, below).

Introduction
Mondadori Archives, Milan: 12, 18, 32 (4); 37a (G. Costa); 16 (G. Lotti); 21 (S. Prato) - Ardea Photographics, London: 32 (3) - Edizioni Agricole Calderisi, Bologna: 32 (1), 33 (7) - Giorgio Lotti, Milan: 14, 15 - Agenzia Ricciarini, Milan: 38 (Emilio F. Simion) - Sally Ann Thompson, Animal Photography, London: 22, 31, 32 (2), 33 (6, 8), 39 - Vision International, London: 33 (5) (Elisabeth Welard)

Photographs at the beginning of each section
Mondadori Archives, Milan (De Biasi): (Light draft, pack and saddle breeds) - Giorgio Lotti, Milan (Ponies) - Agenzia Ricciarini, Milan (opposite title page) - Sally Ann Thompson, Animal Photography, London (Introduction; Heavy draft breeds)

Photographs in the section "Great Champions of Today"
All Sport, London: 243 (M. Powell); 244, 245, 247 (Trevor Jones) - Association Photo, Columbus (Ohio): 251, 252 - P. Bertrand et Fils, Paris: 248, 249 - Equine Images/Harold Roth, New York, 246 - Massimo Perrucci, Milan: 250

Entries
Robin Adshead, London: 120, 123 - Agenzia Novosti, Rome: 54 - Bulgarian Embassy, Rome: 45, 46, 47 - The American Albino Association (White Wings II P501, White Horse Ranch, Nayper/Nebraska): 74 - Animals Animals, Oxford Scientific Films (H. Fox): 169 - Mondadori Archives, Milan: 54 (G. Argent); 171 (C. Shelley); 115, 148, 159 (De Biasi); 132 (G. Dahl, AP); 84 (Hoofs and Horns) - Ardea Photographics, London: 118, 122, 150 - Association National du Poney Landais, Saubisse: 149 - Associazione Allevatori Cavallo Agricolo Italiano (T.P.R.), Verona: 108 - Associazione Nazionale Allevatori Cavallo di Razza Maremmana, Grosseto: 23 - Bob Langrish, London: 16. 17. 79 - Bruce Coleman, London: 85 (J. Taylor) - Color Zenit, Cosenza: 27 (Raf Caputo) - Consejeria de Agricultura, Principado de Asturias, Spain: 152 - Turkish Consulate Milan: 67 - Direktorat Bina Produksi Peternakan, Jakarta: 127, 128, 129, 130 - Don Antonio Ariza Cañadilla, Mexico: 81 - Dr. Glover, Lautem (Island of Timor): 126 - Kit Houghton Photography, London: 76, 162 - Istituto Incremento Ippico, Catania: 29 - Jacana, Paris: 89, 91, 93 (Labat); 94 (S. Chevallier); 151 (J.-P. Ferrero) - Giovanni Lostia, Ozieri: 25, 158 - Manili-Faggiani, Milan: 5b, 24, 88, 153, 156 - Dr. J. Menegatos, Department of Animal Production, Agriculture College of Athens, Greece: 160 - Maria do Mar Oom, Lisbon: 155 - V.M. Nikiforov: 53, 57, 66, 164, 165, 166 - Dr. Giuseppe Ottaviano, Ragusa: 28 - Nova Scotia Government Services/N.S.G.S. Photo: 170 - Massimo Perrucci, Milan: 19b, 70b - Sally Ann Thompson, Animal Photography, London: 1, 2, 4, 5a, 7, 8, 9, 10, 11, 12, 13, 14, 15, 18, 19a, 20, 21, 22, 26, 30, 31, 32, 33, 34, 35, 37, 38, 39, 40, 42, 43, 44, 48, 49, 50, 51, 52, 55, 56, 58, 59, 60, 61, 62, 63, 64, 65, 68, 70a, 71, 72, 73, 75, 77, 78, 80, 82, 83, 86, 87, 90, 92, 95, 96, 97, 98, 99, 100, 102, 103, 104, 105, 106, 107, 110, 111, 112, 113, 114, 116, 117, 124, 131, 133, 134, 135, 136, 137, 138, 139, 140, 141, 142, 143, 144, 145, 146, 147, 154, 157, 161, 163, 168, 172, 173 - Adriano Simonazzi, Collecchio: 69 - Spectrum Colour Library, London: 167 - Ufficio Commerciale Ungherese, Mr. Kovacs, Milan: 41 - Vision International, London: 125 (P. Koch); 3, 6, 36, 101, 119, 121 (E. Welard).